BILL GATES

BILL GATES

A Biography

Michael B. Becraft

GREENWOOD BIOGRAPHIES

 GREENWOOD

AN IMPRINT OF ABC-CLIO, LLC
Santa Barbara, California • Denver, Colorado • Oxford, England

Copyright 2014 by ABC-CLIO, LLC

All rights reserved. No part of this publication may be reproduced, stored in a retrieval system, or transmitted, in any form or by any means, electronic, mechanical, photocopying, recording, or otherwise, except for the inclusion of brief quotations in a review, without prior permission in writing from the publisher.

Library of Congress Cataloging-in-Publication Data

Becraft, Michael B.
    Bill Gates : a biography / Michael B. Becraft.
        pages cm — (Greenwood biographies)
    Includes index.
    ISBN 978-1-4408-3013-6 (hardback) — ISBN 978-1-4408-3014-3 (ebook)
1. Gates, Bill, 1955–   2. Microsoft Corporation—History.   3. Businessmen—United States—Biography.   I. Title.
    HD9696.2.U62G3724   2014
    338.7'61004092—dc23
    [B]   2014017770

ISBN: 978-1-4408-3013-6
EISBN: 978-1-4408-3014-3

18 17 16 15   2 3 4 5

This book is also available on the World Wide Web as an eBook.
Visit www.abc-clio.com for details.

Greenwood
An Imprint of ABC-CLIO, LLC

ABC-CLIO, LLC
130 Cremona Drive, P.O. Box 1911
Santa Barbara, California 93116-1911

This book is printed on acid-free paper ∞

Manufactured in the United States of America

CONTENTS

SERIES FOREWORD

In response to school and library needs, ABC-CLIO publishes this distinguished series of full-length biographies specifically for student use. Prepared by field experts and professionals, these engaging biographies are tailored for students who need challenging yet accessible biographies. Ideal for school assignments and student research, the length, format, and subject areas are designed to meet educators' requirements and students' interests.

ABC-CLIO offers an extensive selection of biographies spanning all curriculum-related subject areas, including social studies, the sciences, literature and the arts, history and politics, and popular culture, covering public figures and famous personalities from all time periods and backgrounds, both historic and contemporary, who have made an impact on American and/or world culture. The subjects of these biographies were chosen based on comprehensive feedback from librarians and educators. Consideration was given to both curriculum relevance and inherent interest. Readers will find a wide array of subject choices from fascinating entertainers like Miley Cyrus and Lady Gaga to inspiring leaders like John F. Kennedy and Nelson Mandela, from the greatest athletes of our time like Michael Jordan and Muhammad Ali to the most amazing success stories of our day like J. K. Rowling and Oprah.

While the emphasis is on fact, not glorification, the books are meant to be fun to read. Each volume provides in-depth information about the subject's life from birth through childhood, the teen years, and adulthood. A thorough account relates family background and education; traces personal and professional influences; and explores struggles, accomplishments, and contributions. A timeline highlights the most significant life events against an historical perspective. Bibliographies supplement the reference value of each volume.

PREFACE

In fewer than three decades, Bill Gates led Microsoft from a start-up in the era of no home computers to almost ubiquitous computing, becoming the world's richest person and using the accumulated wealth to improve the global good.

At the leading edge of the movement toward personal computing, Mr. Gates dropped out of Harvard to become co-founder of Microsoft. Over a period of three decades at Microsoft, Mr. Gates became the world's richest person while serving as a senior executive, technology visionary, and public face of the firm until July 2008, and non-executive chairman from that point until February 2014. Mr. Gates's efforts are now directed toward the Bill and Melinda Gates Foundation, the world's largest charitable foundation. This philanthropic effort is similar to the Andrew Carnegie and Cornelius Vanderbilt charitable focus, using the wealth built over each individual's lifetime.

This book is not intended to be a history of Microsoft nor a history of the Bill and Melinda Gates Foundation, but a concise biography of Bill Gates. His story is inextricably linked to these two organizations, and those organizations will continue to be shaped by him for years to come.

The story of Bill Gates is exceptionally complicated, but the book was written with six major objectives. The first is to illustrate the evolution of Bill Gates from budding entrepreneur to computer programmer to billionaire to philanthropist. Most readers have perceptions of the subject as a billionaire and philanthropist. Second, the book demonstrates that Gates's success was based on a profound understanding of the potential of technology. Third, the book attempts to capture the stages of evolution within Microsoft from inception until the point Mr. Gates left day-to-day control of the company, as this helps us understand how computers moved from objects owned by only the largest of businesses to a nearly ubiquitous item. Fourth, the book takes an approach that recognizes accomplishments as well as failures, praise as well as criticism. In fact, Gates has faced four decades of criticism in some form, despite possessing what many would perceive as traditional measures of success (family, work, accomplishment, and civic engagement). Fifth, the book addresses the motivation of Mr. Gates to use his vast financial wealth to improve the health and education of the poor around the world. Finally, the book attempts to expose the reader to concepts related to the business applications inherent in Mr. Gates's work in global organizations, in nontechnical language and tone.

Along the way, we discover that Bill Gates was—and continues to be—exceptional with positive traits as well as flaws. He was exceptionally fortunate to have been born at the right time to get computer experience and understand at a young age where the industry could go; when he cofounded Microsoft, he was 19. He understood when to take risks and saw many trends in the marketplace, although he also missed many trends along the way. We also see an individual who was competitive, yet always stating that his reason for this competitiveness was the risk of failure; success was never assured in his mind. Gates saw the need for software companies to have firm intellectual property rights and copyrights in the first year of Microsoft's existence and was exceptionally challenging to work for, but also recognized when others provided the most valuable insight. He firmly believed that the products being developed could readily be overtaken by competitors, that he would never have been able to retire from Microsoft if he waited until no competitors would remain, and that work to improve the lives of others with his amassed wealth could be just as rewarding as being the CEO of Microsoft.

ACKNOWLEDGMENTS

Any major activity or undertaking requires the confidence and beliefs of others. I have been exceptionally fortunate throughout my education—formal and informal—to have encountered individuals who have permitted me to gather experiences and skills that many in the United States, and the vast majority worldwide, could not imagine. Out of a persistent fear of omitting someone of critical importance on a list of acknowledgments, I prefer to say "thank you" as I meet each.

I also hope readers know that each of us can be involved in bettering the lives of others in our communities and worldwide with fewer financial resources than Mr. Gates; in the 2014 annual letter released by Bill and Melinda Gates on behalf of their foundation, he states, "If you're looking to donate a few dollars, you should know that organizations working in health and development offer a phenomenal return on your money."

If you are interested in service that greatly improves the lives of others—such as the initiatives of Bill, Melinda, and Bill Sr.—there are dozens of options to commit to helping others. Bill Sr. and I share a common connection as Rotarians involved in the aim to end polio, and Rotary International has participation options for all ages.

TIMELINE: EVENTS IN THE LIFE OF BILL GATES

1955   William Henry Gates III is born on October 28, to William Henry Gates II and Mary Maxwell Gates. As the younger Gates later becomes famous as "Bill Gates," his father eventually adopts the name "Bill Gates Sr."

1968   Bill Gates has his first experience with a computer of the time at his private high school.

1972   The first software partnership of Gates and Paul Allen, along with friend Paul Gilbert, is the Traf-O-Data machine.

1974   Paul Allen sees the January 1975 issue of *Popular Electronics*, which features the Altair 8800.

1975   Gates and Allen move to Albuquerque, New Mexico, to found Micro-Soft, initially writing the BASIC programming language for the Altair 8800; Gates stops attending Harvard to lead the new firm at the age of 19.

1976   Gates writes the *Open Letter to Hobbyists*, his first attempt at protecting the intellectual property of Microsoft.

1977   Microsoft officially becomes a partnership between Gates and Allen, with Gates owning 64 percent of the company.

1978   Microsoft wins arbitration hearing against the maker of the Altair 8800, allowing the company to sell BASIC to many different computer manufacturers.

1979   Microsoft moves to Gates's and Allen's home state of Washington (initially Bellevue, a suburb of Seattle).

1980   In another attempt to protect intellectual property, Gates states that "no one is getting rich" writing software in an interview. Gates hires Steve Ballmer—the person who would eventually become the second CEO—to Microsoft.

1981   The first version of MS-DOS is the operating system for the new IBM PC; the core of the software was bought from another company.

1983   Allen leaves Microsoft after overhearing a conversation between Gates and Ballmer. Gates and Ballmer write the *Applications Strategy Memo*, committing Microsoft to writing for the Apple Macintosh as well as for the PC.

1985   Gates is ranked as one of the 50 Most Eligible Bachelors. Microsoft signs an agreement with IBM to write the OS/2 operating system and releases the first version of Windows.

1986   Microsoft becomes a publicly traded company, and Bill Gates's holdings make him quantifiably rich.

1987   Bill Gates meets Melinda French, whom he would later marry.

1988   Apple sues Microsoft for using the graphical user interface each company had learned about from Xerox PARC.

1989   Bill Gates founds the company now known as Corbis, a venture outside of Microsoft he still fully owns.

1990   Windows 3.0 is released and becomes an immediate success.

1994   Bill Gates marries Melinda French; his mother passes away later in the year. He also purchases the Codex Leicester, the only notebook from Leonardo da Vinci that is owned by an individual (rather than a university or museum).

1995   Bill Gates writes *The Internet Tidal Wave* memo, declaring that the Internet is the most important concept since the IBM PC was released in 1981. Microsoft agrees to a consent decree with the U.S. Department of Justice related to anticompetitive behavior. Windows 95 comes out later that year with Internet Explorer 1.0. Gates releases the first edition of his co-authored best seller, *The Road Ahead*.

1996 Gates releases the second edition of his co-authored best seller, *The Road Ahead*. He and Melinda welcome first child Jennifer Katharine, and he starts his first major philanthropic project.

1997 Bill Gates and Steve Jobs announce an investment by Microsoft in a struggling Apple. The U.S. Department of Justice files a contempt motion against Microsoft from the 1995 consent decree.

1998 While entering a building in Belgium, Gates is hit in the face with four pies. Ralph Nader suggests that Bill Gates and Warren Buffett should convene a conference of billionaires for philanthropic purposes. The antitrust trial against Microsoft begins, with Bill Gates's deposition a critical component of the government's case.

1999 Gates releases his second co-authored best seller, *Business @ the Speed of Thought*. U.S. District Court judge Thomas Penfield Jackson declares Microsoft to be a monopoly. He and Melinda welcome second child Rory John.

2000 Ballmer becomes CEO of Microsoft, while Gates remains chairman and chief software architect. As the legal remedy in the Microsoft trial, Judge Jackson orders a break-up of the firm.

2001 In an appeal by Microsoft, comments made by Judge Jackson against the firm and Gates become public, leading the judge to leave the case.

2002 U.S. District Court judge Colleen Kollar-Kotelly places Microsoft under a new consent decree, without ordering the break-up of the company. Bill and Melinda welcome third child Phoebe Adele.

2004 Gates is elected to the Board of Directors of Berkshire Hathaway, the investment company run by his friend Warren Buffett.

2007 Gates gives the Commencement Address at Harvard University.

2008 Gates has his last day as a full-time employee of Microsoft to focus on the work of the Bill and Melinda Gates Foundation as his primary responsibility.

2010 The Giving Pledge—a group of billionaires who dedicate at least half of their wealth to philanthropic purposes—is initiated by the two people recommended by Ralph Nader, Bill Gates and Warren Buffett.

2011   Immediately after the death of Steve Jobs, the public learns much about the relationship between Gates and Jobs over the past three decades.

2014   Gates resigns from the role of chairman of the board at Microsoft but announces that he will be spending more time at the firm, mentoring the newly appointed third CEO of Microsoft (Ballmer's successor, Satya Nadella) in the role of technology advisor.

Chapter 1

BILL GATES BEFORE AUTOMATED COMPUTING

Well, I was lucky in many ways. I was lucky to be born with certain skills. I was lucky to have parents that created an environment where they shared what they were working on and let me buy as many books as I wanted to. And I was lucky in terms of the timing. The invention of the microprocessor was something profound. And it turned out only if you were kind of young and looking at that could you appreciate what it meant. And then I had been obsessed with writing software. It turned out that was the key missing thing that would allow the microprocessor to have this incredible impact. . . . It is unusual to have so much luck in one life, I think. But it's been a major factor in what I have been able to do.[1]

Upon his birth on October 28, 1955, to a successful family, William Henry Gates III—now widely known as Bill Gates—could easily have been expected to follow in the paths of either of his parents. His father, William Henry Gates II (1925–present), and mother, Mary Maxwell Gates (1929–1994), each were professionals with advanced formal educations. His father was an attorney with a successful practice, which allowed his mother to transition from work as a schoolteacher into other activities with civic and charity impacts.

As relayed by his father, Bill Gates's maternal grandmother and great-grandmother quickly found that a nickname would be required for the younger Gates. A concern was raised that both father and son would be referred to as Bill, which would be overly confusing. As a result, the younger of the two was nicknamed Trey[2] (as in "three" or "third"), and this nickname is still used when father refers to the son. As his son became far better known globally as "Bill Gates" instead of Trey, his father later adopted the name "Bill Gates, Sr.," retiring from his law firm Preston Gates & Ellis in 1998.[3]

Gates's mother was a 1950 graduate of the University of Washington, where she would later serve on the Board of Regents from 1975 to 1993. Originally a schoolteacher, Mary Gates maintained an exceptional level of civic involvement after her husband's law practice became successful. Mary was clearly connected to the University of Washington. Not only did she meet her husband there, but her parents both graduated from the University of Washington. Per a dedication ceremony at the University of Washington after her death, she also served on multiple boards for the university, including the University of Washington Foundation Board, the University of Washington Medical Center Board, and the School of Business Administration's Advisory Board.

> Among her achievements, she served on the board of United Way of King County (1974–88) and many other nonprofit and corporate boards. Her work with United Way led to national recognition of her leadership. She served as a member of the board of directors of United Way International (1980–1990) and was the first woman to chair the executive committee of that board (1985–87).[4]

While serving in the United Way International role, she is reported to have spoken to the chairperson of IBM in a talk that potentially provided support to Bill Gates's software company, which was very small at the time. As Gates frequently recalls in his talks, luck would come into play multiple times in the coming decades.[5]

GROWING UP BILL

His father wrote a book, with a chapter detailing what he learned from Bill and his two sisters. Young Bill Gates was the second of the three children, with one older sister and one younger sister. Older sister Kristi was 10 and Bill was 9, when youngest sister Libby was born. His father noted Bill was usually the last one to the car or be ready for an event, as he was usually in his room reading or thinking. He described Bill as reading almost nonstop, and mentions that his son's competitive nature was likely assisted over the summers by a contest run by his school: "One contributor to Trey's nonstop reading was the fact that every summer the teachers at his school gave their students a summer reading list and there was a contest to see who could read the most books. Trey was so competitive he always wanted to win and often did."[6]

Not only did Bill read an entire set of encyclopedias from front to back, his parents paid for any—and every—book he wanted.[7] Reading for young Bill was connected to another capability his father noted later in life: the ability to read massive quantities and still retain almost all the information from that reading. He wrote that Bill "seems to remember everything he reads and is, at times, eager to share what he's learned with the next person he encounters," and that his son was always intellectually curious.[8] When asked of the best advice he had ever received from his father, Bill stated:

> Well, my dad and my mom were great at encouraging me as a kid to do things that I wasn't good at, to go out for a lot of different sports like swimming, football, soccer, and I didn't know why. At the time I thought it was kind of pointless, but it ended up really exposing me to leadership opportunities and showing me that I wasn't good at a lot of things, instead of sticking to things that I was comfortable with.[9]

AN EXCEPTIONALLY HARD TRANSITION

The experience of the Gates family became much more challenging when Bill Gates was about 11. "The first stage—argumentative young boy—'started about the time he was 11,' Mr. Gates Sr. says in one of a series of interviews. That's about when young Bill became an adult, says Bill Sr., and an increasing headache for the family."

In Robert Guth's words, Gates was "a boy who appeared to gain the intellect of an adult almost overnight" and was challenging his parents on a daily basis, especially his mother.[10] In another interaction, she asked:

"What are you doing?"

"I'm thinking," he shouted back.

"You're thinking?"

"Yes, Mom, I'm thinking," he said fiercely. "Have you ever tried thinking?"[11]

Another day, young Bill was having a nasty argument with his mother at dinner. So his father threw a glass of water into his son's face, to which he responded, "Thanks for the shower."

This was followed shortly thereafter by consultations with a therapist and 12-year-old Bill. And the advice to his parents was to give him more leeway, rather than less, as young Bill would be claiming his independence at some point in the near future. Even today, his father states: "He has very fixed ideas of some things. . . . The dynamic of the family is that you don't cross him on those things, because it's a waste of time."[12]

SEEDS OF CIVIC INVOLVEMENT EARLY IN LIFE

In many works, Bill relates the experiences he encountered while growing up in the Gates family. For instance, he describes extensive volunteer involvement of both of his parents, setting the framework for his later philanthropic efforts but also being exposed to a wide variety of activities, holding discussion in a way that allowed him and his two sisters to be exposed to advanced concepts within those organizations and how decisions were made from a very young age.

> We learned from our parents what they were trying to do, whether it was United Way or a volunteering activity or the world of business. I felt very equipped as I was dealing with adults to talk to them in a comfortable fashion because my parents had shared how they thought about things.[13]

When I was growing up, my parents were almost (sic) involved in various volunteer things. My dad was head of Planned Parenthood. And it was very controversial to be involved with that. And so it's fascinating. At the dinner table my parents are very good at sharing the things that they were doing. And almost treating us like adults, talking about that. My mom was on the United Way group that decides how to allocate the money and looks at all the different charities and makes the very hard decisions about where that pool of funds is going to go.[14]

This civic involvement was present in all three children, although Bill would receive the inclination latest. His older sister, Kristianne Gates Blake, was born in 1954 and owns an eponymous accounting firm, also graduating from the University of Washington like mother and father.[15] She now serves as a regent for the University of Washington like her father: "The biggest lesson I learned from my dad," she said, "is to have a passion for all that you do."[16]

Younger sister Elizabeth (Libby) Gates Armintrout was born in 1964, and served as president of the board at the Lakeside Academy—the same school attended by Bill Gates. She is a board member of the UW Carlson Leadership and Public Service Office and is an active volunteer and contributor.[17]

Each sibling found their own career path but also was involved in service, like their parents. For Kristianne, that was an appointment to the Board of Regents at the University of Washington, and for Libby, that was involvement with Make-A-Wish Foundation, the Lakeside Clinic, the Alliance for Education, and the Susan B. Komen Race for the Cure[18] before becoming a regent for Pomona College.[19] Bill's civic involvement comes decades later but becomes the most important aspect of his life.

Chapter 2

EARLY DAYS IN COMPUTING

Very early in his learning of computers, Bill Gates suddenly found himself involved with a group that solved computing problems for his high school in the late 1960s, when very few organizations had computers and even fewer had the technical capability to actually use computers—programming expertise was essential. It was through this experience that Bill Gates met his first critical collaborative partner—Michael Eisner wrote in *Working Together, Why Great Partnerships Succeed* that Bill Gates always has at least one exceptionally capable partner. From 1968 through 1983, the first of these exceptional everyday partners for Bill Gates was Paul Allen.[1]

At the Lakeside School, he had a lot of opportunities and encouragement from a young age, seeking a means of growth that would give him the independence the therapist stated was coming very soon. He and Paul Allen also had access to a lot of resources that were very rare at that time. For instance, Gates had access to a type of computer that had been invented just a few years before, and the teachers at the school weren't the most capable at programming those computers. In addition to being allowed to read ahead and receiving books from teachers, Gates said of his teachers and school that their ideas on using computers were revolutionary. Rather than allow the computer to be disused (as too confusing), the school allowed the students to take the lead. As Gates said later, "most schools would have just, I don't know, shut the thing down or something."[2]

Bill Gates's first programming experience came in 1968 at Seattle's Lakeside School when the Mothers' Club bought the school access to a time-sharing system. That summer, 12-year-old Bill and his friend Paul Allen, who was two years older, made $4,200 writing an academic scheduling system for the school.[3]

A high school student who wrote the scheduling software for the school could very easily decide which classes he would be placed in. Bill decided to modify the software he and Paul had written to be placed in classes that were entirely filled with girls, which he saw as a clear sign of success for high school students. He later stated, "It was hard to tear myself away from a machine at which I could so unambiguously demonstrate success. I was hooked."[4]

Although he was the youngest on the team of students, he very early established that his involvement in the project would be contingent upon him being in charge of the initiative: "Look, if you want me to come back you have to let me be in charge. But this is a dangerous thing, because if you put me in charge this time, I'm going to want to be in charge forever after."[5]

A criticism of Bill Gates over the decades was that the final responsibility for decisions in settings where he was involved in day-to-day operations rested solely with him. This characteristic has been present in descriptions of Gates from the time he was 12; at times, this attribute was a benefit and at other times a significant failing.

Living up to his father's statements about his son's ability to recall information, Bill Gates is easily able to recount the teachers who had the biggest influence in his early high school days, a testament to their influence on Bill over 40 years ago. In an interview with Serwer, he recalled three of those exceptional individuals from his high school days by name: Fred Wright, Gary Maestretti, and Paul Stocklim.[6]

Success as a computer programmer—in the late 1960s and today—is highly dependent upon a skillset in science, mathematics, and logic. Gates credits his teachers in science and mathematics as key influences

Twenty years after Paul Allen's departure from Microsoft, Gates and Allen speak at a Portland Trail Blazers game; the NBA team is owned by Allen. (AP Photo/ Elaine Thompson)

in his success, simultaneously noting that he ignored the most important aspects of biology due to the poor quality of his high school teacher.

> Well, I think it all comes down to how good the teachers are in 5th through 12th grade. . . . If I hadn't had great teachers during those years I wouldn't have learned how cool science and math are. In fact, I had a bad biology teacher and it's only as an adult that I've realized, hey, biology might be the most interesting science of all. But I stayed away from it. So the science is interesting, and yet it can be made very uninteresting.[7]

And due to this extensive background in science and mathematics, he was able to get the experience he needed with computer software and hardware, at a time when an obsessive level of engagement in an activity of interest was important: "The hard-core years, the most fanatical years, are thirteen to sixteen."[8]

Gates read extensively while in school, learned advanced practices in computer programming before the concept of personal computers existed, and took advantage of the opportunities that were available, both in high school and in computers elsewhere. Although Gates never completed the college degree he started in 1973, he did have a strong educational background from his elite private school, his reading, and his inquisitive nature.

ACCESS TO COMPUTERS

In addition to the computer available at the Lakeside School, Gates did have access to other computers. Most of those computers were based upon time-sharing—having to buy time on computers was what got Bill Gates and Paul Allen into software programming; the pair quickly figured out that their ability to find problems in the software written by others could be used to trade for even more computer time. While Gates and Allen both knew how to program, Allen knew far more about the hardware of the day.[9]

Gates recalled the computers he used at the University of Washington in an e-mail communication much later, and how the University of Washington had unfettered access to a type of computer located at Computer Center Corporation (CCC) that became very important to Gates and Allen in creating future software. At first, the pair started using a computer that required entering data via punch cards, but then they progressed through various buildings, using the resources available. This included calculators, remote computers via teletypes, and even a physically present PDP-10 that the group would use after Paul Allen discovered the computer was available for about six hours per day when it was not processing data. Although those hours were in the middle of the night, Gates wrote that a "friend had a key to the Physics Building so we went up there a lot of times."[10]

Gates and Allen quickly figured out a system where they could have almost unlimited access to computers for experimentation—as long as this was done in the middle of the night when the other processing was completed. The teletype system further allowed the pair to access CCC's computers and run programs by sending messages over the telephone, common in the early days of shared computers with limited processing power. Using the array of machines at the University of Washington helped Gates and Allen learn about solving problems in various languages and operating systems, and led to their first business outside of the Lakeside School.

TRAF-O-DATA

Gates, Allen, and a friend—Paul Gilbert—began work on a project called Traf-O-Data when the Intel 8008 chip was released. In 1972, governments were already measuring the amount of traffic that flowed down streets by placing rubber hoses across a key point, and those hoses were connected to a box on the side of the road. Although this process continues today, the method of evaluating the data has changed substantially. The 1970s' versions of highway traffic measurement had a box on the side of the road filled with a roll of paper tape that was punched with a hole each time a vehicle drove by; those paper tapes had to be unrolled, and traffic counts were calculated by hand.

Allen knew more about computer hardware than Gates but still didn't know how to build a computer that would process the data on the paper tapes. So Paul Gilbert became the third partner. The company would build a computer using the 8008 processor as well as software that would process all the traffic tapes. The plan was to sell this machine to every state and local government as a time and cost-saving tool. Allen had come across a new concept in computer science called emulation; although Gilbert had not yet built their Traf-O-Data computer, Allen wrote a program for the PDP-10s to behave as if the computer was running on an 8008 processor. Effectively, Allen was using the computer access the team had to write software for a computer that had not yet been built. This skill in emulation gave Gates and Allen another big break three years later when the announcement that would lead to the creation of Microsoft was made.[11]

Once Allen had written the software, Gilbert finished building the small computer with a brand new processor. The system was able to process the paper tapes that had previously been processed manually, and the trio was ready to seek their first sale. As Gates's father noted, "after many successful kitchen-table practice sessions my son convinced some employees of the City of Seattle to come to the house for

a demonstration." The tape reader did not work on the day of the demonstration, which frustrated Bill immensely.[12] While the group continued to work on Traf-O-Data, the project was solely passed on to Gilbert
before the one—and only—functional machine was sold in 1975.

As he was closing up his high school years, Allen later recalled how important the development of Traf-O-Data
was to creating their next software initiative: "Even though Traf-O-Data
wasn't a roaring success, it was seminal in preparing us to make Microsoft's first product a couple of years later. We taught ourselves to simulate
how microprocessors work using DEC computers, so we could develop
software even before our machine was built."[13]

As he was closing up his high school years, Gates served as a page in
the Washington State Legislature in Olympia and later as a Congressional page in Washington, D.C.[14]

Yet Gates was still a problem at times for his parents, admitting
that he was exceptionally headstrong and that his father made a
surprising—yet liberating—choice on behalf of his son in high school.
Despite knowing that he was a difficult child for his parents, he was allowed to take time away from high school in order to work: "I got a job
offer and it would take me away from school, and I was amazed that my
dad, after meeting with the headmaster and getting all the data, said,
'Yeah, that's something you can go and do.'"[15]

In his final year of high school, Bill Gates was allowed by his parents
to work full time in computer programming before starting college. The
job he was offered, as a programmer at TRW, is the only time in his life
that he has officially had a supervisor or boss.

In an era where all operations on a computer had to be programmed
by the user, Gates admits that his high school years were when he became addicted to programing. Leaving the Lakeside School and headed
to Harvard, he personally felt that he had already become committed
to being involved in software. While many individuals attend college
and change majors, the admission of being a software person as a law
major creates a potential conflict in purpose. The result was a student
who rapidly completed the advanced mathematics and computing
classes offered by Harvard between 1973 and 1975.

Gates's intellectual curiosity was both a positive aspect and a nega-
tive aspect; like with the example of enjoying the sciences and mathematics, he also described sitting in classes in college where he was not

registered as a student and not attending the classes for which he had registered: "Harvard was just a phenomenal experience for me. Academic life was fascinating. I used to sit in on lots of classes I hadn't even signed up for."[16]

At Harvard, he found the intellectual challenges he was looking for, whether he went to the correct classes or not. Entrepreneurs and businesspeople often share ideas and skills, which lead to many companies in the same industries—or requiring the same skill set—choosing to locate in the same area. Silicon Valley in California is one such example today, where many computer-oriented firms maintain their headquarters. Networks are critical today and were in 1973. It was at Harvard that Gates also met Steve Ballmer, who became his best friend.

"He [Ballmer] was the opposite of me," recalls Gates. "I didn't go to classes much, wasn't involved in campus activities. Steve was involved in everything, knew everyone. Steve was general manager of the football team, head of the lit[erary] magazine, ad manager of the Crimson [newspaper]. He got me to join the Fox Club, a men's club where you put on tuxedos, smoke cigars, drink too much, stand up on chairs and tell stories, play pool. Very old school."[17]

BORN AT THE RIGHT TIME

Was Bill Gates born at precisely the right time to become a leader in the computing revolution? Malcolm Gladwell suggests that he was. Gates and Allen had acquired a tremendous amount of expertise in computers that only the largest firms would possess, knew how to write programs, and had solved problems for other companies in exchange for computer access. In addition, Allen had figured out emulation— how to write software for a computer he did not own (and often had never even seen).

And at the time the story of the Altair 8800 was published in late December 1974 (although listed as the January 1975 issue of *Popular Electronics*), the names that became preeminent in computing—both at Microsoft and at Apple—were all between the ages of 18 and 21. Bill Gates and Steve Jobs were 19, Paul Allen was 21, and Gates's good friend at Harvard University (and his one-day successor at Microsoft) Steve Ballmer was 18, coming off of those fanatical high school years described by Gates:

Bill Gates: October 28, 1955
Paul Allen: January 21, 1953
Steve Ballmer: March 24, 1956
Steve Jobs: February 24, 1955

Malcolm Gladwell also wrote about Gates's good fortune throughout his life, suggesting the combination of Gates's skill and luck could have been replicated if resources were allocated differently. Gates readily admits that he encountered more "luck" than anyone should expect in life. Gladwell noted that "our world only allowed one thirteen-year-old unlimited access to a time-sharing terminal in 1968. If a million teenagers have been given the same opportunity, how many more Microsofts would we have today?"

Nathan Myhrvold, one of Gates's future collaborators at Microsoft and in both versions of *The Road Ahead*, is quoted of the opportunity to pursue writing Altair BASIC:

"If you're too old in nineteen seventy-five, then you'd already have a job at IBM out of college, and once people started at IBM, they had a real hard time making the transition to the new world," says Nathan Myhrvold, who was a top executive at Microsoft for many years. "You had this multibillion-dollar company making mainframes, and if you were part of that, you'd think, Why screw around with these little pathetic computers?"[18]

Along with close partner Paul Allen, Gates had to make a choice when the MITS Altair was introduced, along with the 8088 chip that was inexpensive and was capable of allowing home computers, first among smaller groups of users called "hobbyists."

At the time, the Altair 8800 was designed to just show results in a series of 16 LED lights and had 16 switches to enter data. That Altair qualified as a computer in 1974/1975, even without an operating system or programming language available. Users had the opportunity to purchase external terminals (or build their own) to operate like rudimentary monitors for the products, or even use a telephone to connect directly to a more powerful, time-sharing computer.

If an individual were to purchase the Altair 8800 Minicomputer in 1975, the first step would have been to assemble the parts of the computer itself. No monitor, keyboard, or mouse; the assembly process would have included the individual boards, connectors, and switches within the case. The next step would have been to either test the computer or begin to write programs in the language of the time. Using only zeroes or ones to type in the entire computer program, this was not a user-friendly process. For instance, the following steps were listed in the February 1975 issue of *Popular Electronics* to tell the computer how to take two numbers (one from input channel 6 and one from input channel 30), add those two numbers, and then return the sum result in output channel 128.

Table 2.1—published in *Popular Electronics*—was to suggest that the revolutionary Altair was user-friendly in allowing one to add two

Table 2.1 Machine Instructions

Instruction	Binary Code	Octal	Comment
IN 6	11011011 (IN)	333,006	Bring data from input 6 And store in register A(accumulator).
MOV B,A	01(MOVE) 000 (B) 111 (A)	107	Take A and move its contents to B.
IN 30	11011011 (IN) 00011110 (30)	323,036	Bring input 30 into accumulator.
ADD B	10000 (ADD) 000 (B)	200	Add contents of A to B. Put results in A.
OUT 128	11010011 (OUT) 10000000 (128)	323,200	Transmit contents of accumulator to output 128.

Source: Re-created from *Popular Electronics*, February 1975, p. 58.[19]

numbers. In fact, one of the proposed uses for the Altair was to build one's own scientific calculator, a device that costs a few dollars now without the need for programming expertise. In 1975, a device that was solely used for scientific calculation was very expensive.

In order to see the potential for widespread use of a system such as this, one had to be a very clear visionary. There were multiple people who saw the potential of this system, including Bill Gates, Paul Allen, and the early employees of Microsoft (originally called Micro-Soft) who were willing to work for Gates's upstart firm. The system and chip also drew the attention of Steve Jobs, who went on to become a founder of Apple with Steve Wozniak using different hardware.

So why was the Altair so important for early computing? In January 1975, the minimum wage increased to $2.10 per hour.[20] A basic mini-computer like the Altair 8800 was still rather expensive as a discretionary purchase at $397. However, this was a major jump in affordability in terms of computing, and individuals could have their own computer at home for the very first time. The Altair cost less than $397 and could fit on a desk, the PDP-10 was the size of a refrigerator and cost almost $20,000, and the early teletypes Gates and Allen had used required leasing time at $40 per hour. Comparatively, the Altair was extremely affordable.

DROPPING OUT OF HARVARD TO WORK ON THE ALTAIR

Although it is common knowledge that Gates dropped out of Harvard to work on the MITS Altair, he did not drop out until his partner Paul Allen had demonstrated that the Altair BASIC worked and had secured a contract from MITS. With the benefit of hindsight, Gates was able to admit that the company he and Allen founded could have been delayed, probably for another year or so. Of the fear of missing out on the opportunity presented by the Altair:

> In our case, Paul Allen and I were afraid somebody else might get there before us. It turned out we probably could've waited another year, in fact, because things were a little slow to start out, but being on the ground floor seemed very important to us.[21]

However, Gates and Allen did not know at the turn of 1975 that the early days of their firm would be slow. So why did Gates and Allen feel that immediate action was required? The founder of MITS had been hearing from a lot of people about developing a version of the BASIC programming language that was a small enough file that it would function on the Altair's limited memory. Like most items Gates was able to commercialize over his life, the concept of the BASIC programming language already existed; someone just had to figure out how to make it work on the limited space available on the Altair and be the first to do so:

> He (*Ed Roberts of MITS*) was getting ten calls a day from people who had a BASIC "almost ready," and his stock response was, "The first person who shows up with a working BASIC gets the contract."
>
> Gates and Allen had never seen an Altair; they had never even seen the Intel 8080 microprocessor at the heart of the Altair. But a couple of years earlier Allen had written a program on a mainframe computer that emulated the operation of a previous Intel microprocessor, and this time around they did the same thing.
>
> With an Intel 8080 manual at his side, Allen sat down at a Harvard PDP-10 computer and wrote the emulator and software tools necessary to do the programming. Meanwhile Gates stopped going to classes and devoted himself to designing the BASIC, using every trick he knew to get the size down below four kilobytes.[22]

With this urgency placed, Gates and Allen were now attempting to rush through the development of a programming language for a computer neither had seen, for a processor they had never touched, without the ability to test on that computer model or processor along the way. Writing the software based upon Allen's emulator skills alone—without the ability to test—was a large leap of faith but necessary in the minds of the two young developers. If others were actively working on Altair BASIC, their opportunity would be gone if their project was not finished first. Eventually—in the coming days or the very near future—someone was going to develop Altair BASIC, and the first one to the finish line would benefit.

Why was the 4-kilobyte restriction so necessary for the Altair? In the early days of computing, processor power and speed were far below even basic electronic devices we see today. Four kilobytes was the technical limitation of the computer chip. In order to first run the BASIC programming language and then any program written in BASIC, there had to be space left in what was a very limited memory capacity. The 4-kilobyte restriction would require writing all parts of the BASIC programming language in under 4,000 characters, where letters, numbers, spaces, and punctuation marks all counted as characters. And the Altair 8800 had no operating system, so the BASIC had to function as both the operating system and the programming language: "At the time Altair BASIC was written no operating systems, good or bad, existed so it had to be stand-alone."[23]

As a point of reference on the limited amount of characters Gates could use, imagine typing an essay today with a *total* of about 50 lines of text; that's how much space Gates had to write his version of the entire programming language that also served the function of the operating system (like Windows today): "The finest pieces of software are those where one individual has a complete sense of exactly how the program works. To have that, you have to really love the program and concentrate on keeping it simple, to an incredible degree."[24]

As Gates mentioned himself in *The Road Ahead*, second edition, the combination of having a microcomputer available, at a reasonably affordable price, with an acceptable chip but no software was an opportunity he did not see lasting very long. With no programming languages available, it was not a useful tool although Gates and Allen saw the potential future. He even went so far as to suggest that he and Allen had a bit of panic at the time:

What the Altair did have was an Intel 8080 microprocessor chip as its brain. When we saw that, panic set in. "Oh no! It's happening without us! People are going to go write software for this chip." The future was staring us in the face from the cover of a magazine. It wasn't going to wait for us. Getting in on the first stages of the PC revolution looked like the opportunity of a lifetime, and we seized it.[25]

Actually, Gates and Allen—the pair—had to seize the opportunity, although the part about Allen was omitted in the first edition of *The Road Ahead* but was "corrected" for the second edition. Others suggest there was more than a fear about the development of the Altair. In fact, Gates was described in *Microsoft Rebooted* as paranoid someone else would take the lead on writing a version of BASIC for Altair, noting:

Lacking software, the Altair could not be programmed, depriving it of practical value. To perform more complicated tasks, the Altair needed a user-friendly programming language. Gates and Allen decided to pursue the writing of such a language even though one mini-computer firm had argued that it was impossible to write a high-level language that would run on a personal computer.[26]

Once Allen had demonstrated the Altair BASIC and the software worked, the pair had a choice. Gates realized that if his company were to grow once the Altair BASIC was available, he would have to leave Harvard, and soon:

We realized that things were starting to happen, and just because we'd had a vision for a long time of where this chip could go and what it could mean didn't mean the industry was going to wait for us while I stayed and finished my degree at Harvard.[27]

Allen was already living near his friend Gates in Boston but was not a student at Harvard. He was working as a programmer at Honeywell after dropping out of college himself; he had already completed two years of college and entered the workforce as he was two years older than Gates. By the standards of an era, Allen had landed a job with an industry giant:

Drifting at Washington State, I was ready to take a flier. I mailed my résumé to a dozen computer companies in the Boston area and got a $12,500 job offer from Honeywell.[28]

A move to support their version of Altair BASIC would impact both, and the way to support the Altair would most likely require a move to be near MITS. Bill Gates decided to take a leap of faith, although a very difficult choice. In 1975, at the age of 19, he stopped out of Harvard to cofound Micro-Soft, dropping out completely the next year. As a result of this choice, Gates took control of the company from the first day. According to Gates, Allen's money for the startup came from working at Honeywell, while some of his own money to fund the start-up company had come from playing poker at Harvard.[29]

FAMILY PERCEPTIONS OF
THE COLLEGE DROPOUT

"Gates's parents were devastated. His mother was 'very, very apprehensive' about his future, says his father."[30] In his own book, Bill Gates Sr. noted, "Of course, Mary and I were sick when Trey told us he planned to leave college to take advantage of a window of opportunity he believed would be long gone by the time he graduated from Harvard. However, he promised us that he would go back to Harvard, 'later' to get his degree."[31]

The precise circumstances of Gates's final departure from Harvard are a little unclear, and some have suggested the true reason for Gates's departure was disciplinary rather than willing choice. While it is well known that Gates and Allen worked on their Altair BASIC during Gates's time at Harvard, there is some debate as to whether Gates left the school voluntarily or was subject to administrative pressure, discipline, or reprimand from the university. Given the U.S. federal law that protects student records (FERPA, or Family Educational Records and Privacy Act) passed in 1974, the university will never be able to state whether Gates was subject to any form of discipline.

At question was the use of the computers at Harvard by Gates and Allen for a potential commercial purpose. The question is whether the pair was indeed using a computer paid for by the government in an attempt to make a personal profit. Given the cost of using computers at the time—$40 an hour—and that the funding for the computer time was coming from the federal government, this could be seen as an inappropriate use of a government resource.

In an 1998 article by Golden and Yemma for *The Boston Globe*[32] about fund-raising efforts that resulted in a donation of $15 million from Gates to put his mother's name on a new facility (she had passed in 1994), the writers even quoted Gates's father as suggesting that there was some form of conflict between Gates and the administration of Harvard:

> Gates has said that he withdrew from Harvard to pursue his career. However, according to interviews, he left after a dispute over alleged rules violations at the Aiken lab, including using its computers for private business.
>
> "There was a flap, no question about it," says his father, William Gates Sr., who now runs his son's charitable foundation. "My son felt a little put upon by the Harvard administration's attitude."
>
> Gates lived in Currier House at Radcliffe, but the Aiken lab was his true Harvard home, where he often worked through the night. His troubles began when a lab administrator discovered that Gates was using the Aiken computer to write computer code for a New Mexico company. Because the federal government was funding the computer time, the administrator felt that Gates was misusing not just a Harvard facility but also public funds.

Later in their article, they describe much of the motivation that Gates would possess to continue involvement with Harvard in the future, despite never earning a degree from the institution. While Gates had become widely successful and grown a company from the beginning of an industry into a name known around the world, he always understood failing to meet his family expectations of completing his degree. The desire to name a facility after his mother was initiated out of his acute awareness of that perceived failing: "After Gates's mother, Mary Maxwell Gates, died in June 1994, Rudenstine (Harvard official) sent a sympathy note. According to sources, Gates responded that his mother's greatest disappointment was that he had not graduated from Harvard."[33]

Gates never did earn a degree at Harvard, although he returned to the university on two very notable occasions. The first time was in a speech to a group in 2004, when he inspired Facebook cofounder Mark

Zuckerberg, in the audience. The second time was when he gave the Commencement Speech in 2007 and was awarded an honorary doctorate by the university. Although his mother had passed away 13 years before and his degree was honorary rather than earned, he was able to joke about the "promise" he had made to his father: "I've been waiting more than 30 years to say this: 'Dad, I always told you I'd come back and get my degree.'"[34]

For a college dropout, Bill Gates believes extensively in the value of a college education as a basic credential needed to succeed in the workplace today. While he indeed never finished college, he does believe that a college degree today is a basic requirement for employment, much like a high school diploma was at one time. His success as a billionaire entrepreneur without a college degree is not easily copied, although there are a limited number of individuals—including in the technology sector—who meet that characteristic (Paul Allen of Microsoft, Steve Jobs of Apple, and Mark Zuckerberg of Facebook are examples). Later in life, he would get involved in educational initiatives at all grade levels through a charitable foundation, always stressing that he had received an exceptional education despite leaving college early and that a college degree was a minimum credential to promote future success.

Chapter 3

EARLY DAYS OF MICROSOFT

Gates would not have been able to succeed at Microsoft without his partnerships and talented people. He confirmed that in a talk much later in life, when he said that the single best business decision he had ever made was going into business with Paul Allen in 1975, followed by hiring his Harvard friend Steve Ballmer. Gates and Ballmer—who joined the company in 1980—pushed Allen out of the firm by early 1983: "In my case, I'd have to say my best business decisions have had to do with picking people. Deciding to go into business with Paul Allen is probably at the top of the list, and subsequently, hiring a friend—Steve Ballmer—who has been my primary business partner ever since."[1]

On Gates's and Allen's 1975 move from Cambridge, Massachusetts (home of Harvard) to Albuquerque, New Mexico (home of MITS, the maker of Altair), historian Paul Ceruzzi wrote, "Their move set in motion not only the founding of one of the country's biggest corporations, but it also led to the digital computer moving from its initial place as an expensive, specialized device affordable only by big businesses, government agencies, or scientific labs, to a technology that has spread first to the desktops and now the pockets of consumers around the world."[2]

The company was named Micro-Soft (with the hyphen, and later with no space) at the suggestion of Paul Allen, because the company was making "microcomputer software" instead of working on large mainframe computers. So the firm had a name that would remain with limited variation over time. At the founding in 1975, the company's address was in Albuquerque, New Mexico, at 819 Two Park Central Tower.

His parents were not very sure of this business venture controlled by their son. At the time, the Gates family did believe that Bill would return to Harvard one day. And in the early days of Microsoft, there were many tenuous times when the business was indeed capable of failing. The company was attempting to start an industry from a computer that was seen by others as difficult to use and only acceptable to a user with very precise knowledge of how computers worked at a fundamental level. These people were called hobbyists; micro-computers were a hobby rather than an occupation.

When Microsoft was founded, Bill Gates was very young (age 19). However, he needed to be self-convinced that the development of the firm would be beneficial to himself and he also needed to have the ability to persuade others that his vision for the future was practical. For Gates, Allen, and the friends who decided to join Microsoft at the founding, there was significant uncertainty: working to develop a new industry as well as the change of setting from the familiar state of Washington or Harvard University in Massachusetts to the city of Albuquerque, New Mexico.

Starting a new business in an entirely new industry was more than a little daunting. The earliest Microsoft employees were Gates, Allen, and many of their friends. How does a 19-year-old convince friends that his vision of the software would lead to a successful firm?

> There become a few magic moments where you have to have confidence in yourself. . . . When I dropped out of Harvard and said to my friends, "Come work for me," there was a certain kind of brass self-confidence in that. You have a few moments like that where trusting yourself and saying yes, this can come together—you have to seize on those because not many come along.[3]

That "brass self-confidence" is seen as a characteristic of the *Masters of Enterprise* as conceptualized by H. W. Brands. Of the 25 masters he identified—and Gates was one—the commonalities were good health and abundant energy, hunger and passion for the work, a close and intense identification with work, the ability to persuade others to buy into their personalization, and a creative vision.[4] People did follow Gates, and he was the public face of Microsoft for many years; many still associate him with the firm despite leaving all day-to-day operations in 2008.

Along the way, the CEO of this new small business—after convincing his friends to accept job offers—had to worry about paying those same friends. In the early days of Microsoft, the cash flow to pay employees was sometimes imperiled.

> The thing that was scary to me was when I started hiring my friends, and they expected to be paid. And then we had customers that went bankrupt—customers that I counted on to come through. And so I soon came up with this incredibly conservative approach that I wanted to have enough money in the bank to pay a year's worth of payroll, even if we didn't get any payments coming in. I've been almost true to that the whole time.[5]

Gates believed that the move from Harvard to start a software company was time-sensitive. Others who saw the same issue of *Popular Electronics* may be actively looking to develop software, and some of these new software developments would be based upon copying the software made by Microsoft. This created a number of rationalizations within his mind; the protection of his corporation's intellectual property would always remain important and Microsoft would have to create exceptional new innovations in order to succeed over the long term.

> There certainly were a lot of other software companies. Within two or three years of our being started, there were dozens of companies. Some of them tried to do better BASIC. And we made darn sure they never came near to what we had done. There were competitors in other languages. They didn't quite take the same long-term approach that we did, doing multiple products, really being able to hire people and train them to come in and do great work, taking a worldwide approach, and thinking how the various products would work together.[6]

Bill Gates was always contemplating the future in some way. And even though the Altair was a box without even a programming language in early 1975, Gates had an idea of the future that involved using computers for reading, note-taking, and other tasks: "The early dream was a machine that was easy to use, very reliable, and very powerful. We even talked back in 1975 about how we could make a machine that all of your reading and note taking would be done on that machine."[7]

Of course, this was a challenge given computers of the day, where all calculations and operations had to be programmed once a language like Microsoft's Altair BASIC was written, using very precise syntax. Without Microsoft's Altair BASIC, every single character—letter, number, or space—had to be entered in by hand, with a series of 0s and 1s; eight switches had to be flipped for every character printed. In order to get to a point where average people would be able to conduct reading and note-taking on a computer, there would be a number of major evolutionary steps required.

First, someone had to create an operating system for the computer, such as the version of DOS—Disk Operating System—that Microsoft provided to IBM in the early 1980s. The Altair already had a rudimentary operating system, which required programming in binary (the 0s and 1s). Today, Windows is the operating system that is associated with Microsoft. Second, software companies had to create programming languages for each computer, such as the Altair BASIC that was the original focus of Microsoft; while this was the initial focus of the company, few computer users actually use programming languages today. Microsoft's earliest expertise is still present on every computer, although not commonly used by those who purchase a computer with Microsoft software. Finally, the software companies had to create applications for that operating system that would be intuitive enough for the average user. Applications like Microsoft Office are taken for granted today and are how the vast majority of computer users know their computers, yet these were missing in the earliest days of computing. Gates and Allen wrote the programming languages—the second part—so individuals could write their own applications. Microsoft has evolved to being known for every part of the chain except the part that led to the firm's founding.

Combined, these steps took very few years from the founding of Microsoft in 1975, although the operating system we know now as Windows, with graphics and the ability to click/select icons, did not come into being for almost a decade. In fact, Apple was a much bigger company than Microsoft until the introduction of Windows. And Gates was not alone in his 1975 vision of using computers in the way described back in 1975; Xerox's PARC (Palo Alto Research Center) had been founded in 1970 based upon a belief of a paperless office *coming by the year 1990*.[8] Although Xerox had an incorrect idea of the future, its work at PARC greatly influenced the industry. Xerox—which had started as a photographic company but made its biggest impact on the world through the introduction of the photocopier—was greatly worried about a world where paper was no longer needed. Later, Xerox would influence Apple and Microsoft into developing a lot of the innovations still used in computers today, like graphical displays and computer mice or pointers.

SUCCESS BASED UPON QUICK TURNAROUNDS

We didn't even obey a 24-hour clock, we'd come in and program for a couple of days straight.[9]

In the early days of software development, the *early mover advantage* was critical. The first company to create a product that could be marketed would develop easy partnerships with other firms (as Microsoft did with MITS). With the same urgency that led Gates to leave Harvard in order to found Microsoft, we also see that the company was necessarily committed to working long days to meet deadlines with the hardware providers to whom they had made commitments. Time became an abstract concept for the employees of the company shortly after founding, with Gates actively involved in programming projects.

Gates and Allen were among the earliest to recognize that computers would become everyday appliances and had a shared vision of the capability of the programmers at Microsoft. However, Gates greatly misunderstood the global scope of computing and the number of employees that would be needed at the firm as the growth rate of the firm accelerated. Not only did Gates personally know many of the earliest employees, he had also hired these individuals. And Gates firmly believed that a company of 100 people—or fewer—could create enough software to supply the entire global market. This underestimation meant that the firm quickly grew past the point where Gates could know all the employees, and even all the managers of products under development at Microsoft.

> We thought the world would be like it is now in terms of the popularity and impact of the PC, but we didn't have the hubris to think that our company would be this size or have this kind of success. The paradox is that we thought, "OK, we can just have this 30 person company that will be turning out the software for every PC."[10]

> If you had asked me at any point how big Microsoft could be, Paul and I once thought we could write all the software in the world with 100 people.[11]

Gates also understood that at the founding of Microsoft, the key players in the industry were all about the same age. Malcolm Gladwell also noted this characteristic in his book *Outliers*, where the major players in Microsoft and Apple were all born in a very short timeframe, around the age of 20 when these two firms were formed to become major enterprises based upon a piece of technology that could change an industry. In fact, Gates didn't recall working with anyone over the age of 30 in the early days of micro-computing, a statement reiterated by Apple's Steve Jobs at an event in 2007:

> "It's funny," says Bill Gates. "When I was young, I didn't know any old people. When we did the microprocessor revolution, there was nobody old, *nobody*. They didn't make us meet with journalists who were old people. I didn't deal with people in their 30's. Now there's people in their 50s and 60s. And now I'm old and I have to put up with it."[12]

Microsoft was married to MITS, creating various versions of BASIC for specialized purposes by necessity; the firm could not make versions of BASIC for other companies until other companies decided to make micro-computers requiring BASIC. This meant that the early success of Microsoft was solely driven by how many copies of Altair BASIC were sold by MITS, as Microsoft only received a percentage of each license that was sold. Soon, Gates would fight his first battle to protect Microsoft's intellectual property, as he learned that MITS was selling very few licenses for Altair BASIC.

THE OPEN LETTER TO HOBBYISTS

More than 25 years before Napster was shut down to comply with a court order about copyright infringement, Bill Gates faced his own issues in protecting intellectual property. The firm founded by him and Paul Allen had written the Altair BASIC programming language that was sold by MITS. Computers at the time were limited in scope to major research institutions and small groups of individuals called hobbyists. Bill Gates noticed that less than 10 percent of all Altair computer purchases had an accompanying sale of Altair BASIC to run on the computer.

Effectively, the vast majority of users of Altair BASIC had used the software without ever purchasing a license to do so. This upset Bill Gates, who crafted an open letter that was mirrored by many artists and performers 25 years later in the cases against Napster and other peer-to-peer file sharing services (which were clearly illegal by the year 2000, copying software was not clearly illegal in 1976), raising many salient questions. If a software company is not compensated for costs required to develop the software, would that prevent other individuals and organizations from undertaking the effort to develop the software to make computers truly usable?

Gates and Allen had taken a significant risk in starting Microsoft, feeling that personal computers would be absolutely meaningless without good software. As he notes, even with the Altair BASIC his company created, the computer still required programming skills to use—the average consumer could not (yet) effectively use the device. Based upon his company's revenues he was able to determine that for each 10 Altair computers purchased, less than one license for his company's Altair BASIC was being purchased. At the same time, he was getting enthusiastic notes and feedback from more BASIC "users" than the number of licenses MITS had sold.

As a software company, his firm clearly benefits from the sale of licensed copies. This relates to the concept of marginal cost in economics; the initial development costs are very high but the cost of selling additional copies of the software is very low. However, the corporation could fail if the development costs of the software are never made back by selling licenses. Gates recognized that with the amount spent on developing the versions of BASIC, the revenue to his company was less than $2 per hour, about half of the minimum wage at the time. If his product development costs consistently exceeded the cost of his employees' time and labor, Microsoft would likely rapidly fail, and there would be little incentive for other companies to develop software for computers. Furthermore, he declared that those computer hobbyists who used the software without purchasing were guilty of theft, also identifying a nuance of the software market at the time. While more than 90 percent of the users were not buying the official software through MITS, some of the users were paying for unofficial software from people who had copied the software without putting any time or effort into the development process. Of this group, he had particular disdain, stating "They are the ones who give hobbyists a bad name, and should be kicked out of any club meeting they show up at."[13] He invited suggestions (and payments) to an apartment address in Albuquerque, New Mexico. The apartment in question still exists, near Kirtland Air Force Base and the city's commercial airport (now called the Albuquerque International Sunport), and the text of the letter—as printed in many of the magazines and newsletters available to computer users in 1976—is available through many forms of electronic media.

Fun fact: People did write to Bill Gates (now age 20) and a few even included a check for the cost of Altair BASIC. Most assuredly, Gates would not include his mailing address on a communication sent to computer users today.

While Gates was insistent that Microsoft should be compensated for the time and effort placed into developing the software, he was incorrect on a major conceptual component in the letter. At the time, copyright protection in the United States did not extend to computer programs, so anyone copying his software was technically not infringing on his copyright (and thus not a thief), although selling a copy made might be against the law in an individual state.

A legal case in 1976 might be created based upon a state's "unfair competition" laws. Those laws—when available in a state—would apply only to a business or individual who was making a profit by reselling the work of Microsoft. The aspect of making a profit was key; members of the clubs who were giving away copies clearly would not be deriving a profit, and thus were not competitors. And unless an individual had signed a nondisclosure agreement specifically with Microsoft or MITS (selling Microsoft's products), there would be no violation of trade secrets. The ability of Gates—and the leaders of all other software producers—to gather profit from producing and selling software in the 1970s was imperiled. Given a total of 60,000 Altair computers were sold over the lifetime of MITS, the ability of Microsoft to sell its BASIC to a higher percentage of users was critical to the firm's survival.[14]

EARLY ADOPTION OF POWER

While Microsoft started in 1975, Gates and Allen officially formed their partnership on February 3, 1977. According to Allen, the agreement contained two very important clauses. While the agreement was between only two people, there was a clause that a partner would not have to work if attending school as a full-time student and another clause that in an irreconcilable dispute, Gates could force Allen out of the firm.[15] Gates had the majority stake in the firm with 64 percent of all the shares, was clearly the controlling partner in Microsoft, and still—even at some low level—considered the possibility of returning to Harvard in the future.

Gates also understood early on the power of a single operating system to allow other organizations in the computer hardware and software industry to work effectively together. As early as 1977, he spoke about having one standard operating system for computers to make the job of computer programmers much easier. At the time he made the statement in writing, he did not know that he was speaking of *his own* company's future; he believed a standard operating system would be desirable (like Windows today), but his company was not focused on writing operating systems. In fact, his company had not even written an operating system at the time he wrote that the industry would benefit from a single OS:

> The best thing for users would have been if all the manufacturers of personal computer hardware had got together years ago and decided on a standard OS. Every time a new device was introduced the driver needed in the standard OS would have to be included with the hardware. Software houses would write programs to run under the standard OS and wouldn't have to worry about multiple versions. The source of the OS would be widely available and everyone could make suggestions for its enhancement.[16]

Gates wasn't selling MS-DOS, Windows, or Microsoft Office at the time; those products did not exist as of yet and that was not Microsoft's market. Gates's company was one of the software companies that developed programming languages only; he had never hired anyone with expertise in operating systems or applications. In fact, Microsoft was still four years from "developing" its own operating system, where "developing" meant "purchasing from another company." Yet according to Cringely, Gates consistently would state "we want to monopolize the software business" in the 1970s.[17] At the time, Gates was still in his early 20s, and Microsoft was small. Once Microsoft was large enough to have a public relations staff, he was probably counseled against stating that he wanted to form a monopoly, as that usually draws the attention of the federal government.

DISPUTE WITH MITS THREATENS THE COMPANY

Microsoft's growth was constrained by a dispute with Altair builder MITS over license agreements and the total amount of royalties, as Ed Roberts was trying to sell his company. This created a very possible failure point for the company, as Microsoft was looking to sell modified version of the BASIC programming language to other competitors, while MITS was attempting to take ownership of the full rights to the Altair BASIC developed by Microsoft. Losing access to the one product created by the firm would have spelled the end of Microsoft in 1978, many years before Windows was created. MITS had a judge enforce the arbitration clause in the original contract, which meant that Microsoft was in a critical holding pattern. The company was not receiving any revenue from MITS, the company was paying lawyers, and the company was forbidden to sign contracts until the arbitrator made a decision. When the arbitrator finally decided, Microsoft was able to sign many contracts with other vendors previously negotiated, and take all of the money from those contracts, without revenue-sharing with MITS.

> By the beginning of September, the arbitrator sent down word in no uncertain terms: MITS had violated the agreement in what Paul Allen remembered the arbitrator calling "one of the worst cases of corporate piracy I've ever seen." Although MITS could continue to sell Microsoft's 8080 BASIC for its own machines, its exclusive license was officially terminated. MITS would no longer share in future third-party royalties, and Microsoft was free to sell the product to all comers.[18]

At this point, Microsoft's future looked much brighter. The company didn't have to share any revenue from sales of Altair BASIC with MITS, owned the complete rights to its software under the contract, and could sign all the agreements that were placed on hold during the arbitration hearing. This sudden inflow of cash saved the firm and started another key pattern of Microsoft under Gates's leadership; as Microsoft was not building the actual computers, he was willing to sell revised versions of BASIC for every company that did decide to build computers. Even early Apple and Commodore computers ran a version of BASIC written by Microsoft. Customizing one product for every participant in the early market for micro-computers provided Microsoft the revenue to grow, and soon relocate from Albuquerque. Microsoft would not begin to work on operating systems or applications in earnest until after the move to the state of Washington, first in Bellevue in January 1979.

Working at Microsoft was never easy, and many early employees left. Of the Albuquerque dozen a few weeks before the move to Washington—11 people immortalized in the December 7, 1978, company portrait plus a 12th person who missed the photo due to a snowstorm[19]—Bill Gates and just two others would still work at the firm in the 1990s.[20]

INTELLECTUAL PROPERTY WHEN NO ONE IS GETTING RICH

After the *Open Letter to Hobbyists* in 1976, Gates had hoped the issue of copyright had been solved by revisions to copyright laws. He was sadly mistaken. The laws on copyrights had been modified slightly since Gates wrote the widely disseminated *Open Letter to Hobbyists* in February 1976, within the first year of Microsoft's existence. However, Gates and Microsoft were still in an important battle to protect their intellectual property. The 1980 interview with Dennis Bathory-Kitsz was incorporated into an article called *Have the Courts Smashed Software Copyright?* in 80 *Microcomputing* magazine. The magazine was named after the TRS-80 computer, which also used a form of BASIC written by Microsoft. And Gates understood that the current model of software being used endemically without licenses created little incentive to pay for a licensed copy:

There's nobody getting rich writing software that I know of.[21]

In an interview where Gates strictly defended the rights of his firm to protect Microsoft's intellectual property from being copied, he truthfully—at the time—described the state of the industry as not being particularly lucrative for the developers of software. He had already learned from his experiences with competitors and users when his only product was Altair BASIC. Given no legal disincentive to using the software written by Microsoft without buying licenses, the company's product would be copied and/or resold without the firm receiving a commission on those sales. In order for Microsoft to grow, there was a need for a substantial change in the way the intellectual property of software was treated by the government of the United States, although those same protections would come much later in some of the markets entered by Microsoft.

The year 1979 was a critical point for software developers in the early age of computing. In fact, many software developers thought the interpretation of laws had taken a step backward. The revisions to copyright laws in 1976 had asked for a commission (*CONTU*, or *Commission on New Technological Uses of Copyrighted Works*) to write a report about software stored on various electronic media and whether photocopies violated copyright; the commission had suggested a process such that software would be covered by copyright. Although Congress had not yet acted on the report from the commission, many assumed that the issue had been resolved for computer programs. Then a firm named JS&A was sued for selling a product called "JS&A Chess Computer," which was an exact replica of Data Cash's "Compu-Chess" product. Although JS&A was selling software created by another firm, a federal judge ruled in 1979 that copying and selling the program did not violate copyright law at the time.

Given his stance in the *Open Letter to Hobbyists* just four years previously, the thoughts of a 24-year-old Bill Gates on the issue were very predictable. If a precedent-setting ruling from a federal judge stated that software stored on electronic media was not protected by copyright, there would be few legal mechanisms available to stop any computer program from being copied, re-labeled, or resold without any revenue to the creator of the work. Widespread copying of software quickly became prevalent, and Bathory-Kitsz noted, "Stated very simply, the copyright laws, the most general form of protection for authors and artists, may not apply to the final version of programs as prepared and sold on magnetic media—disks, tapes, wafers—or in read-only-memories (ROMs)."[22]

At the time of the *Open Letter*, Bill Gates noted that $40,000 was spent in developing the Altair BASIC. Microsoft had grown from that time, and expenses in software development were far greater. Without the ability to use patents or copyrights, he described how Microsoft tried to protect the company's products. "We spend millions of dollars a year creating software programs, and we are protecting those in several ways. There's the trade secret laws where we get non-disclosure—that's how we handle our source codes and our so-called commercial packages that are high-priced." Yet not all software was high-priced, and Gates still believed "if the law wasn't going to protect it, there wouldn't be any software written," consistent with the *Open Letter*.

When informed by Bathory-Kitsz that someone had taken source code created by Microsoft and republished the material elsewhere, Gates was insistent that his rights had been violated. "He certainly has because that's my material. Whose does he think it is? Does he think that he has the right to go out and commercially profit by republishing something that we created? I mean, that's ludicrous! Why should he be making money from that? All he did was take our stuff."[23]

Although this was Gates's second major round in protecting the intellectual property created by Microsoft, it would not be the last. The issue with federal copyright law gets resolved within a few years, whereas charges of unfair competition and violation of intellectual property did arise in the future, including charges against Microsoft and other firms controlled by Bill Gates.

HIRING PERSONNEL TO GROW

As the 1970s rolled over into the 1980s, Gates recognized that his company would benefit from hiring superstars in computer science and software development. He also recognized the converse; if the best programmers he had already attracted started to leave the firm, then others would as well. Microsoft had to become a destination for the most exceptional programmers, despite being a small company when compared to the likes of Apple or IBM. And the demanding Gates was clear that his employees had to be very talented, where the vast majority of the population would be unqualified for his work: "The key for us, number one, has always been hiring very smart people. There is no way of getting around, that in terms of I.Q., you've got to be very elitist in picking the people who deserve to write software. Ninety-five percent of the people shouldn't write complex software."[24]

Gates's reputation for being a challenging boss is well earned. As a software programmer himself, he clearly understood that the majority of people should not be involved in developing new software. The key understanding of Gates was not that software developers need to graduate from the most prestigious colleges; neither he nor Allen had graduated from college at all. He did know that software developers should consistently be high IQ individuals.

1980—Hiring Steve Ballmer

The second of Bill Gates's exceptional everyday partners was Steve Ballmer, from 1980 through near the present day, overlapping with Paul Allen from 1980 through 1983 in Eisner's model.[25] First, Gates had to convince Ballmer to join the firm as the business manager, in an era when Gates was already known for both his technical capability and controlling knowledge of everything done by his firm. Waters wrote decades later that the young Gates:

> once ruled Microsoft with a command of detail and intellectual intensity that led to the kind of culture that was capable of dominating the tech world—even as it tipped over into behaviour that brought a regulatory backlash. "I was a kind of hyper-intense person in my twenties and very impatient," he says. "I don't think I've given up either of [those] things entirely."[26]

In 1980, the young Gates had very little measured intensity. He was simply intense. Persuading Steve Ballmer to come to Microsoft was an undertaking. Although a long-time friend of Gates, Ballmer was in graduate school at Stanford after getting his baccalaureate degree in mathematics and economics at Harvard.[27] So Gates worked somewhat on impressing Ballmer in the recruitment and interview process, even bringing in his mother and father for an assist: "Inviting Ballmer to Seattle, Gates wined and dined his college friend, getting him together with his parents, Bill Sr. and Mary, and giving him a tour of the city."[28]

The recruitment and interview process was a high priority of Gates but not his highest priority at the time. Years later, Ballmer would reveal that Gates left for vacation during the interview; Gates already knew who he wanted at the company.[29]

Ballmer also received partial ownership of the company to come to Microsoft on June 11, 1980. As the first business manager of Microsoft, the market would see the first IBM personal computers launch a year later, each running MS-DOS, the first commercial operating system for PCs. Gates then realized that hiring exceptional programmers would be the next step in growing Microsoft. And in his case, he started by hiring Dr. Charles Simonyi from Xerox PARC—the group that had been working on advanced computing techniques starting in 1970 because Xerox feared the paperless office that could occur by 1990.

> Gates knew that attracting very good programmers made it easier to attract others of the same caliber. Stars sought to work wherever the best in their fields congregated. Gates in 1981 had recruited Charles Simonyi from Xerox PARC as one of the first "really bright guys I hired in software development." The presence of Simonyi, who can be regarded as the father of Microsoft Word, in turn helped to lure others. This was only one of the many virtuous cycles that were the centerpiece of Gates's management philosophy. The converse was also true. If Microsoft were to lose its best programmers, others would begin thinking about leaving, too. Thus Microsoft had to pay ongoing attention to retention as well as recruitment.[30]

Like with the example of Traf-O-Data, where Allen knew far more about hardware than Gates, Bill was at a decision point for Microsoft. Although he had been programming extensively for the firm in terms of programming languages, he "knew very little about applications and admitted it."[31]

Even much later, Gates recognized the importance of his most talented employees among a staff of thousands, saying "Take our twenty best people away, and I will tell you that Microsoft would become an unimportant company."[32] Although reported as exceptionally demanding, Gates understood that he needed to attract and retain the highest-quality employees in a company of exceptionally bright people.

1981—Selling an Operating System Requires an Operating System, IBM and QDOS

Bill Gates had a connected family and likely benefited from those connections in the earliest days of Microsoft. His mother was on the board of the United Way of America at the same time as the chairman of International Business Machines (IBM). That company was looking to develop a computer that would be affordable to home users but not compete with the cherished, high-profit commercial market. And Microsoft was fortunate, as there were two projects where the suspected lead candidate did not win. Per the obituary of Mary Gates, she may have provided Microsoft's most critical connection:

> In 1980, she discussed with John R. Opel, a fellow committee member who was the chairman of the International Business Machines Corporation, the business that I.B.M. was doing with Microsoft.
> Mr. Opel, by some accounts, mentioned Mrs. Gates to other I.B.M. executives. A few weeks later, I.B.M. took a chance by hiring Microsoft, then a small software firm, to develop an operating system for its first personal computer.
> The success of the I.B.M. P C gave Microsoft and its MS-DOS (for Microsoft Disk Operating System) a lift that eventually made it the world's largest software company for personal computers.[33]

Microsoft was still specializing in programming languages at the time, including FORTRAN, BASIC, and COBOL. IBM started by asking Microsoft for BASIC, which Microsoft was already selling to everyone else. Gates even made the recommendation on what chip IBM should use for the computer.[34] IBM asked for an operating system, and Bill Gates knew of a firm—and a programmer—that IBM did not know about.

After securing the rights to provide a Disk Operating System (DOS) to IBM, Microsoft and Bill Gates encountered a significant quandary. The company had never before developed an operating system for a computer, focusing on programming languages instead. In a business sense, Gates had a choice between three very different alternatives in order to meet the IBM deadline. The firm could develop the operating system internally with existing programmers, the company could acquire another firm with the expertise to develop an operating system, or the company could essentially buy the rights to an existing operating system that was not used on other devices.

At the time, few people understood the importance of the IBM product that was being created. Bill Gates was one of the individuals who did understand the importance. For IBM, with a long-standing interest in mainframe computers rather than reaching household consumers, the project was not envisioned for the revolution that it would cause. Not only would IBM-PC compatible computers quickly overtake Apple computers in the home market, but Microsoft would benefit by being able to sell a single product to IBM as well as IBM's competitors.

On July 27, 1981, for the amount of $50,000, Microsoft bought the complete license for the product developed by the Seattle Computer Products called 86-DOS (previously QDOS—Quick and Dirty Operating System). While the purchase agreement was signed by Microsoft vice president and cofounder Paul Allen, the official point of contact for all inquiries from that date forward was "William H. Gates" at Microsoft's Bellevue, Washington address. The IBM PC was introduced two weeks later, on August 12, 1981, and Microsoft had complete rights to the operating system used on the prevalent 8086 computer processor at the time. What had been called "86-DOS Disk Operating System for the 8086—Version 0.3"[35] was now Microsoft's MS-DOS, and Microsoft had a product that would lead to phenomenal revenue growth.

The contractual Agreement of Sale between Seattle Computer Products and Microsoft contained resolution for some issues related to intellectual property that had plagued Microsoft in the early days and discussed and described by Bill Gates, both in the *Open Letter to Hobbyists* and the later interview in *80-Microcomputing*. Seattle Computer Products was allowed to continue selling copies of the operating system along with processors, paying a royalty to Microsoft for each computer sold in a legally binding contract. Most notably, all purchasers of a product with the operating system now owned by Microsoft had to sign a "Registration and Non-Disclosure Agreement" that precluded the ability to copy the software without violating the trade secrets of Microsoft, specifically:

> The party above named and below signed agrees that it is receiving a copy of the above named software for use on a single computer only, as designated on this registration form. The party agrees to fill out and mail this registration form to MS before making use of

the software. The party agrees to make no copies of the reference software except for the purpose of backup for the above specified computer and to strictly safeguard the original software and backup copies against disclosure to persons not specifically authorized by MS. The party further agrees that unauthorized copying or disclosure of this software will cause great damage to MS and Seattle Computer Products and that this damage is far greater than the value of the copies involved.[36]

Microsoft had clearly made an intentional move to say that computer software was associated with a single computer, and that the operating system necessary for using the computer was inherently tied to a single machine. As the number of computers in place throughout the world increased, this would become a very lucrative business model: one that eventually begins to draw the attention of competitors and the U.S. Department of Justice.

The day the IBM PC was announced was a critical point in the history of Microsoft. If one had an invitation to the IBM press conference and were looking for Bill Gates the day the PC with MS-DOS was announced, he would not have been seen. He was not at the IBM ceremony, as the device was not seen as important enough to invite anyone at all from Microsoft, no less the CEO of the firm. On the day of the IBM announcement in 1981, Gates happened to be at Apple headquarters. Of the personnel at Apple looking at the announcement: "They didn't seem to care," he said. "It took them a year to realize what had happened."[37]

The IBM press conference described the innovation of the PC, with a brief mention of Microsoft. Students could now write papers, businesspersons could use accounting software, and the manuals provided meant that almost anyone could start using the computer *within hours*, and then begin personalizing their own programs. The computer was still about a decade away from the ability to simply plug in, turn on, and use:

IBM has designed its Personal Computer for the first-time or advanced user, whether a businessperson in need of accounting help or a student preparing a term paper. An enhanced version of the popular Microsoft BASIC programming language and easily understood operation manuals are included with every system. They make it possible to begin using the computer within hours and to develop personalized programs quite easily.[38]

Why was this event such an important event in the history of Microsoft? Almost all of the 500,000 computers running the previous operating system (CP/M) were replaced by 10 times as many computers running MS-DOS.[39] This was a tremendous deal for a Gates-led Microsoft; he revisited the same business model as he had with BASIC. Any time a new manufacturer wanted to compete against IBM, he had a customized version of MS-DOS available. And now that he had an expert in developing applications, each manufacturer buying a customized version of MS-DOS could also purchase applications customized to the customized MS-DOS. Effectively, Gates could sell a slightly different operating system and slightly different applications to every computer manufacturer, including Apple. No matter which manufacturer ultimately succeeded, Microsoft would get paid.

Immediately after the release of MS-DOS on the IBM PC, there was trouble on another project for which Gates was providing a version of BASIC, the TRS-80 Model III. In the confusion as to whether Radio Shack or Microsoft was the primary contributor to the problem, Gates received the reputation of being nonresponsive at times. Even in 1981, that elicited the statement "Bill Gates (president of Microsoft) is notorious for not being reachable by phone and for not returning phone calls."[40]

1982/1983—CRITICAL ILLNESS OF ALLEN

In 1982, with the company located in a Seattle suburb, the leaders of Microsoft were honored by the Lakeside School with the Distinguished Alumni Award; Gates was in the high school class of 1973 and Allen in the class of 1971.[41] Later that year, Allen was diagnosed with a form of lymphoma that could have caused his death at a young age if not treated aggressively.

During his recuperation, cofounder Allen was slowed in his work due to chemotherapy treatments. He overheard a talk between Bill Gates and Steve Ballmer in December 1982. As Allen relayed himself in *Vanity Fair*, Gates and Ballmer were conspiring to reduce Allen's ownership of the company without his involvement, and Allen was not pleased. Back in 1977, Microsoft was found as a partnership where Gates could remove Allen from the firm at any time. That partnership agreement was no longer in place—Microsoft became a corporation on June 25, 1981—and Allen could hold on to his ownership interest in the company as long as he wanted, even if he chose to leave.

Allen notes Gates as trying to end the year 1982 with an olive branch, writing in a note on New Year's Eve, "During the last 14 years we have had numerous disagreements. However, I doubt any two partners have ever agreed on as much both in terms of specific decisions and their general idea of how to view things." The next month, Gates and Allen exchanged offers to buy out the departing Allen's shares in the firm. Allen rejected Gates's initial offer, Gates rejected Allen's counter-offer, and Allen left the company with his shares of Microsoft stock.[42]

With Allen's offer to sell his shares at a set price rejected by Gates, most would think the interaction was detrimental to Allen. In fact, Allen was exceptionally fortunate. The buyout of his portion of the company would have netted a few million dollars if Gates had accepted Allen's price. Microsoft's explosive growth came much later, which made Allen a billionaire while he was off pursuing other interests, at his own pace, to protect his post-lymphoma health. Borsook labeled Allen the "accidental billionaire" and wrote "his wealth is a lucky trick of time and place, and particularly of his involvement with Bill Gates. While Allen was co-responsible for the early creation and early technical successes of Microsoft, his tremendous wealth came later. Gates made them both billionaires after Allen left off an active involvement with Microsoft."[43]

1983—GATES AND MEMORANDUMS TO STAFF

June 1983 saw a famous memorandum that was co-written by Bill Gates and Steve Ballmer. This was the Applications Strategy Memo, which told staff that Xerox PARC's vision was the future of Microsoft, and that the existing operating systems—those without graphics or mice— would not be developed in the future:

Microsoft believes in mouse and graphics as invaluable to the man-machine interface. We will bet on that belief by focusing new development on the two new environments with mouse and graphics . . . Macintosh and Windows.

. . .

Microsoft will not invest significant development resources in new Apple II, MSX, CP/M-80 or character-based IBM PC applications. We will finish development and do a few enhancements to existing products.[44]

What was most insightful about this message? That not only was Microsoft going to be working on Mac applications and then Windows, but that the Macintosh applications would actually be developed first.

The Mac was a very, very important milestone. Not only because it established Apple as a key player in helping to find new ideas in the personal computer but also because it ushered in a graphical interface. People didn't believe in graphical interface. And Apple bet their company on it, and that is why we got involved in building applications for the Macintosh early on. We thought they were right.

—Bill Gates[45]

1983—GATES'S INTELLECTUAL PROPERTY WIN WAS ACTUALLY BY APPLE

Gates had maintained from the creation of his firm that the software created was his work, and should be protected under copyright protection. Despite the revisions to the law governing copyright in 1976, the legal setback in 1979 that suggested electronic media was not covered persisted a few more years until 1983. And the case that finally put to rest the idea of copyright wasn't about the software developed by Gates or Microsoft, but software developed by Apple. August 30, 1983, was the significant date in the case *Apple Computer, Inc. v. Franklin Computer Corporation*, which was sent to the U.S. Court of Appeals Third Circuit after an adverse ruling against Apple in the same case three days prior.

Franklin attempted a novel defense in the case when Apple presented evidence that the software used was almost identical to that used in the Apple II. In fact, Franklin had not even bothered to change some references to Apple and Apple employees encoded in the software, so denying the copies would be impossible. As noted in the court opinion comparing the Apple II and Franklin's ACE 100 computer:

> Apple produced evidence at the hearing in the form of affidavits and testimony that programs sold by Franklin in conjunction with its ACE 100 computer were virtually identical with those covered by the fourteen Apple copyrights. The variations that did exist were minor, consisting merely of such things as deletion of reference to Apple or its copyright notice. (5) James Huston, an Apple systems programmer, concluded that the Franklin programs were "unquestionably copied from Apple and could not have been independently created." He reached this conclusion not only because it is "almost impossible for so many lines of code" to be identically written, but also because his name, which he had embedded in one program (Master Create), and the word "Applesoft," which was embedded in another (DOS 3.3), appeared on the Franklin master disk. Apple estimated the "works in suit" took 46 man-months to produce at a cost of over $740,000, not including the time or cost of creating or acquiring earlier versions of the programs or the expense of marketing the programs.[46]

And the changes Franklin made were exceptionally minimal, such as changing the eight letters that spelled "Apple II" when booting the computer to instead read "ACE 100." So what was Franklin's defense that was promptly rejected by the judge at the appeals court? Franklin argued that operating systems would not be covered by copyright, and that copying Apple's operating system was further permissible because Franklin did not have the capability of developing its own similar operating system: "Franklin did not dispute that it copied the Apple programs. Its witness admitted copying each of the works in suit from the Apple programs. Its factual defense was directed to its contention that it was not feasible for Franklin to write its own operating system programs."

The judge promptly rejected Franklin's contention that an operating system was not covered by copyright. And Bill Gates immediately knew how important this ruling was for Apple, Microsoft, and all other firms developing various software applications and operating systems; in fact, Microsoft was extensively involved with many providers, including Apple. Gates took the opportunity the next month to write a celebratory "Opinion" piece that was published in the *New York Times*. Gates knew that if Franklin had won, then the future of Apple, Franklin, and Microsoft would be imperiled by copies of their software freely made by companies in other countries. He celebrated that the court had ruled "all computer software, whether it appears on a floppy diskette or is etched into the silicon chips deep inside a computer, is protected by United States copyright laws." Gates had been claiming for years that software development would (eventually) stop in the United States without the protection, and that courts in Europe had already decided that software could be copyrighted. Gates noted that the software industry was still nascent and computers would be easier to use given more investment by the various competitors in the market. He also described a very fragmented industry, with thousands of competitors—not a limited few competitors—working to reach the market with their software: "Imagine the disincentive to software development if after months of work another company could come along and copy your work and market it under its own name . . . . Without legal restraints on such copying, companies like Apple could not afford to advance the state-of-the-art."[47]

At this point, there was room for Apple's Jobs and Microsoft's Gates to celebrate; the U.S. judicial system had finally—for good—decided the software critical to each firm's success was protected.

As PCs were taking off and millions of new users were becoming familiar with MS-DOS, Gates participated in a 1983 Apple event that was set up as a game show. In one of the many contradictory public statements he made over time, he described the Macintosh to be released in January 1984 as the most revolutionary idea. That Macintosh initiative was being led by Steve Jobs and Gates said:

to create a new standard takes not just making something that's a little bit different, it takes something that's really new and captures people's imagination. And the Macintosh, of all the machines I've ever seen, is the only one that meets that standard.[48]

Microsoft was also working on a project for IBM-PCs in 1983. It was called "Windows."

1984—The original Macintosh was released on January 24, 1984, with an iconic commercial shown a few days before during the Super Bowl. Microsoft was firmly connected with Apple, Gates was developing ideas for Windows, and Apple and Gates were both building off the work at Xerox PARC, which had not been able to make innovations related to a paperless office into a successful business.

> They showed that it was easier to instruct a computer if you could point at things on the screen and see pictures. They used a device called a "mouse," which could be rolled on a tabletop to move a pointer around on the screen. Xerox did a poor job of taking commercial advantage of this groundbreaking idea, because its machines were expensive and didn't use standard microprocessors. Getting great research to translate into products that sell is still a big problem for many companies.

Microsoft CEO Bill Gates in 1984 (age 28 or 29), nine years after the founding of the firm. (AP Photo)

We worked closely with Apple throughout the development of the Macintosh. Steve Jobs led the Macintosh team. Working with him was really fun. Steve has an amazing intuition for engineering and design as well as an ability to motivate people that is world class.

It took a lot of imagination to develop graphical computer programs. What should one look like? How should it behave? Some ideas were inherited from the work done at Xerox and some were original.[49]

As 1984 was drawing to a close, Gates was again supporting the Macintosh in the media over the IBM PC.

Chapter 4

DEVELOPMENT OF PRODUCTS
USED TODAY (1985–1998)

1985—ELIGIBILITY (DATING AND BUSINESS PARTNERSHIPS)

In early 1985, Bill Gates was rated by *Good Housekeeping* magazine as one of the "50 most eligible bachelors."[1] There was at least one error in the magazine's description; he was 29 years old rather than the listed 28.

In June 1985, Microsoft signed a Joint Development Agreement with IBM to make an operating system called OS/2, signed by William H. Gates on page 43.[2] Microsoft did the development but was also working on versions of Windows in the background. So we have Microsoft selling MS-DOS to anyone making a computer similar to an IBM, software to Apple, an operating system to IBM, while working on its own operating system and selling applications to any consumer with a checkbook. No matter who wins this round of the technology evolution, Microsoft will again profit.

Although Windows was announced in 1983, the first release came on November 20, 1985. Microsoft had become known for quick turnarounds on projects, so some computer experts began to believe that

Windows was *vaporware* in the years between the announcement and the release. The term vaporware has many connotations—it can be a product the company wants to release but became a lower priority or not technologically feasible. Vaporware can also be a product that was never intended to exist, in which case it is announced to confuse competitors or nudge a competitor out of the market. As Microsoft announces: "On November 20, 1985, two years after the initial announcement, Microsoft ships Windows 1.0. Now, rather than typing MS–DOS commands, you just move a mouse to point and click your way through screens, or 'windows.' Bill Gates says, 'It is unique software designed for the serious PC user.'"[3]

Apple did not think Windows 1.0 was unique enough. And Steve Jobs was no longer at Apple, although he would return in 1996. The company had hired a CEO to be the business face of Apple in 1983; John Sculley was famously recruited by Jobs with the line, "Do you want to spend the rest of your life selling sugared water, or do you want a chance to change the world?" The Macintosh did not meet sales projections and the battle between Jobs and Sculley led to a battle where Jobs was left with no team. In fact, Jobs took the removal of his staff as being fired in a very harmful way:

> I was out—and very publicly out. What had been the focus of my entire adult life was gone, and it was devastating.[4]

Jobs was "devastated" for part of 1985 but recovered quite well. He responded by starting another computer company called NeXT and a computer-based animation company called Pixar, which would create many popular movies three decades later. And those responses meant his path with Apple—and with Microsoft—would intersect again.

1986—MICROSOFT SELLS STOCK AND BECOMES PUBLICLY TRADED

In 1986, Microsoft became a publicly traded company and thus everyone could buy and sell shares in the company at will. For Gates, this was a major change in a company he had firmly controlled for more than a decade already; he would now be accountable to others who had queries about Microsoft stock. And he was not happy about the prospects, although selling shares of stock would allow Gates to take money out of Microsoft whenever he wished:

> "The whole process looked like a pain," he recalls, "and an on-going pain once you're public. People get confused because the stock price doesn't reflect your financial performance. And to have a stock trader call up the chief executive and ask him questions is uneconomic—the ball bearings shouldn't be asking the driver about the grease."[5]

So why does a firm decide to become publicly traded on a stock market, especially a firm where the chief executive officer (Gates) had expressed little desire to be involved in a process allowing individuals or businesses to call and ask about the company and the company's prospects? There are multiple reasons for becoming a publicly traded company.

On the initial sale of stock by Microsoft to the public, the firm would receive a substantial inflow of cash. The amount of that inflow would be the product of the number of shares sold times the price per share (less a commission to the banking firms that helped sell the shares). Acquiring cash through a stock sale can be viewed as safer than acquiring cash through borrowing money (debt), which would require periodic interest payments. While there would be more owners of the firm—a share of stock is a partial ownership of the firm—the company would now be able to use the cash raised from the initial stock sale to make investments that allow expansion and new products.

A side effect of becoming a publicly traded company, with a listing on a stock exchange, is that the founders or existing owners now have an easy way to sell part—or all—of their ownership in the company. The founders of Microsoft, such as Gates and Allen, immediately held shares of stock that were worth many millions of dollars as part of the initial public offering (IPO) process. These shares can be sold by the major executives of the firm in the future, as long as those executives follow rules that prevent individuals with insider knowledge from trading shares on upcoming good (or bad) news.

MICROSOFT AS AN INCREDIBLE
WEALTH GENERATOR

In order for a corporation to grow, the products or services offered by the corporation have to be desired by customers (whether business or individuals). For the first 11 years of Microsoft's existence, the company was very closely held and never had issued an IPO, which means there were no shares of stock issued that could be bought and sold readily. The average investor could not purchase stock in Microsoft until the official IPO on March 13, 1986, when a single share of MSFT stock sold for $21. Shares of Microsoft can still be bought or sold by individuals on the NASDAQ stock market under the symbol MSFT.

Microsoft used the proceeds from selling the IPO shares at a fortuitous time in the development on technology for businesses of all sizes as well as consumers. Due to the rapid creation of wealth in the firm, one share bought on the first day Microsoft was available would have grown to 288 shares if held for the entire growth spike in Microsoft's first 25 years as a public company.[6] Like many fast-growing companies, Microsoft issued routine stock splits to keep the price accessible to more investors. The extensive growth in computing—and Microsoft—in this era made many Microsoft investors and employees quite wealthy.

The growth of the company made Bill Gates—the largest shareholder and CEO—an exceptionally wealthy individual, often listed as the wealthiest person in the world over the past two decades. In fact, the position of wealthiest individual in the world has only been held by three people over the past two decades: each year, the listing has been topped either by Bill Gates, his good friend Warren Buffett (of Berkshire Hathaway), or Carlos "Slim" Helu (of Mexican telecommunications firm América Móvil).

OS/2 AND WINDOWS 2.0 RELEASED

The first version of OS/2 was released in December 1987 per the agreement with IBM. The second version of Windows was also released in December 1987. Both of these products were written by Microsoft, so the firm again benefitted no matter which product was more successful.

In 1988, Gates suggested that OS/2 could be the most important operating system of all time, another intrinsically contradictory statement:

> I believe OS/2 is destined to be the most important operating system, and possibly program, of all time. As the successor to DOS, which has over 10,000,000 systems in use, it creates incredible opportunities for everyone involved with PCs.[7]

Microsoft, under Gates, was a clear beneficiary of having multiple "most importants," considering he had extolled the virtues of MS-DOS, Apple's MacIntosh, Microsoft Windows, and now IBM's OS/2. Independent of which platform became dominant Microsoft would benefit and continue to grow as long as the market for home computers continued to grow.

APPLE COMPUTER INC. VERSUS MICROSOFT CORPORATION

In 1988, Apple filed a lawsuit against Microsoft based upon the use of the graphical user interface (GUI) in the Windows operating system. Bill Gates was not amused, and his relationship with the new Apple CEO (Sculley) was not as strong as his relationship with Jobs.

A step back in history reminds us that Steve Jobs (of Apple) and Bill Gates (of Microsoft) were not the originators of the GUI that was the focal point of the lawsuit. In fact, both learned about the concept of a GUI from Xerox's Palo Alto Research Center (PARC). Xerox, as the owner of PARC in the 1970s, examined its strategic options in the market for operating systems and did what any potential rights owner of that invention would do.

Xerox filed a copyright lawsuit against Apple the next year. Industry observers immediately thought that 1989 was a little late, as the Macintosh was no longer a "new" item on the market. Why would Xerox not file a lawsuit against both Apple *and* Microsoft? That was a simple business matter. Microsoft never claimed ownership of the idea of the GUI, while Apple was attempting to own the rights to the concept. If the courts decided that Apple "owned" the rights to all operating systems with a GUI, Apple would receive licensing revenue for what had been an idea developed by Xerox. This scenario took a while to sort out; Xerox sued Apple for using its invention, while Apple sued Microsoft for ostensibly stealing an idea both firms derived from Xerox.

This story has roots that had gone back at least three years. Steve Jobs had been pushed out of influence at Apple by John Sculley and the board of directors. And Sculley didn't like the idea that Microsoft would be releasing Windows 1.0. Even years later, Gates's disdain was apparent in talks with Jim Carlton related to the first legal nudges before the lawsuit. Carlton captured the thoughts of both Gates—who knew of the same GUI at Xerox PARC as Steve Jobs saw in November 1979—and Charles Simonyi, the software application expert Gates had specifically hired from Xerox PARC. Gates knew that both companies had been similarly inspired, and that Apple intentionally withheld information that would have been trade secrets to actually be within dispute.

> Gates was hopping mad. He had not stolen anything from Apple, he insisted then and continues to insist now. The whole idea of GUIs had originated not with Apple, he points out, but with Xerox. "The father of the Mac is Xerox. The father of Windows is Xerox," Gates says. Charles Simonyi, Microsoft's in-house GUI maestro, compares the similarities between Windows and the Macintosh to those found in different automobile models. "When you decide to build an automobile, you're not going to change the steering wheel," Simonyi says. "They all have common ancestry. This was such a silly and pointless argument that they were falling into."[8]

No one ever disputed that the idea of a GUI came from Xerox. If Xerox had immediately sued, the outcome might have been different. Xerox lost the case against Apple, Apple lost the case against Microsoft, and the escapade ended in 1994, with each of the three firms spending a lot of money on lawyers but essentially making no progress.

MICROSOFT WAS USING E-MAIL IN THE 1980s

In a 1988 interview with *Success Magazine*, Gates noted that Microsoft was already using electronic mail: "We have electronic mail here—that is, we send messages to each other electronically over our computers. So, if you have a brainstorm all of a sudden, you can send your idea out immediately, and only to the people you think should be involved."[9]

SMALL-MARKET WINDOWS 3.0 IS A BIG SUCCESS

On May 22, 1990, Windows 3.0 came out, rapidly surpassing sales of OS/2. In 1992, Gates noted that OS/2 became an IBM-only initiative: "We always thought the best thing to do is try and combine IBM promoting the software with us doing the engineering. And so it was only when they broke off communication and decided to go their own way that we thought, okay, we're on our own, and that was definitely very, very scary."[10]

At some time near this point, Microsoft adopted an HR practice called stack ranking, which the company confirmed as being in place for multiple decades when cancelled in 2013. Under that evaluation system, supervisors had to grade every team member on a ranking scale from 1 to 5, and a predetermined proportion of team members had to be rated as unacceptable. This practice was described later as leading to dysfunction among teams and high-achieving workers intentionally avoiding work with other high achievers, specifically to avoid the possibility of low rankings.[11]

In 1993, there was debate whether Microsoft was too powerful. Gates describes the market for server hardware: "'This is a hypercompetitive market,' Gates says. 'Scale is not all positive in this business. Cleverness is the positive in this business.'"[12]

He goes on to note that due to the cost of development, applications were now generating more profit than operating systems, although that was only a very recent pattern in Microsoft's history. Windows 3.0 in 1990—the product that relegated OS/2 away from Microsoft into an IBM-only project—was the operating system that brought Microsoft Word to the mass market. Even a former IBM executive who became the CEO of another firm commented at the time that the fear of Microsoft in the software market should dissipate over time: "Today, everyone is in fear of Microsoft. But in the end, everyone will compete. There are thousands of Bill Gateses out there who will find pieces of this market and win them."[13]

Bill Gates with Intel CEO Andy Grove in 1993. Microsoft's software runs extensively on Intel processors. (AP Photo/Barry Sweet)

THE INTERNET (WHICH MAY BE A TIDAL WAVE)

Microsoft's awareness that something very dramatic was going on around the Internet really came from employee[s] . . . so he became a change agent at Microsoft . . . And people looked at that, they looked at the other memos they had saying similar things, and we said, boy, this is profound.[14]

On May 26, 1995, Bill Gates sent forward an e-mail memorandum called "The Internet Tidal Wave" to the executives of Microsoft and the staff who reported to him directly. In that memo, Gates made some very strong claims about the implications of the Internet and Microsoft. In many respects, he was correct while assigning the Internet "the highest level of importance," going forward to say the "Internet is the most important single development to come along since the IBM PC was introduced in 1981." For a company known extensively for operating systems, that would be a huge development. And he clearly understood the concept of reinforcing feedback in terms of what would lead to an explosion in the growth rate of Internet use, stating that he believed almost all computers would be used to connect to the Internet and: "Most important is that the Internet has bootstrapped itself as a place to publish content. It has enough users that it is benefiting from the positive feedback loop of the more users it gets, the more content it gets, and the more content it gets, the more users it gets."[15]

He got some aspects of the Internet entirely wrong. Although he saw that HTML would dominate, he thought that other existing protocols, "FTP, Gopher, IRC, Telnet, SMTP, NNTP," would still be used. Most personnel in the computer industry have not used four of those six protocols since shortly after Gates's memo in 1995 (if ever).

What bothered Gates most about using the Internet early in 1995? Even before the founding of Google, he said "it is easier to find information on the Web than it is to find information on the Microsoft Corporate Network." While surfing the Internet of 1995, he did find a lot of Apple QuickTime files online for movie advertisements, as well as Adobe PDF files—even the government was using them—but not a single file type with a Microsoft extension (e.g., a Word document).

And then there was Netscape, where Gates wanted to get people to switch to Microsoft's alternative, saying "we need to offer a decent client (O'Hare) that exploits Windows 95 shortcuts. However this alone won't get people to switch away from Netscape." O'Hare, we find out later, was Microsoft's code-name for the very first version of Internet Explorer. And he also talked about Blackbird, which was intended to be an alternative to the HTML pages we see on the web daily (although he already conceded that HTML would be the standard).

Gates also mentioned a specific fear. And that was common in his talks throughout time. Even when Microsoft was market-dominant, he did not believe that the success of the company was fully assured. He believed the Internet could lead to the generation of very cheap products that would essentially allow for limited capabilities like the browsing of the Internet: "One scary possibility being discussed by Internet fans is whether they should get together and create something far less expensive than a PC which is powerful enough for Web browsing."[16]

Funny that Gates should mention the possibility of a PC alternative that would be far cheaper and have the capability of using the web. While basic computers with Windows 95 capability started around $1,000, the idea of an alternative had already been postulated by Larry

Ellison, one of the other stars of the early days of micro-computing, CEO and cofounder of Oracle software:

> "Here's what I want," said Ellison. "I want a $500 device that sits on my desk. It has a display and memory but no hard or floppy disk drives. On the back it has just two ports—one for power and the other to connect to the network. When that network connection is made, the latest version of the operating system is automatically downloaded. My files are stored on a server somewhere and they are backed up every night by people paid to do just that."[17]

Consumers did find a product similar to the one Gates feared in 1995 and that Ellison had mentioned. The product just took 18 more years to arrive, with the Google Chromebook that did not run Windows, updated automatically, stored information in the cloud, and was a cheap means of connecting to the Internet for approximately $200, rising from a "negligible" share of the reseller notebook market in 2012 to 21 percent in 2013.[18]

Windows 95 was the first version of Windows that a user would associate with Windows today. The product was released on August 24, 1995, and was one of the largest product launches in history. Gates took the stage to introduce the brand new operating system, and avoiding the marketing campaign was all but impossible. In fact, Segal noted that the advertising campaign for Windows 95 was believed to be the single largest advertising campaign in history through that point in time, with rumors suggesting that the Rolling Stones made a fortune simply for licensing one of their songs for the product launch: "Twelve million dollars was spent simply securing the rights to a theme song for the hoopla, the opening chords of the Rolling Stones hit 'Start Me Up.'"[19]

At the time, Segal noted exceptionally costly marketing campaign could be risky, and implied that expensive launches have been accompanied by massive failures in the past, including the Ford Edsel. He also passed along the rumor—ostensibly started by the Rolling Stones— that Microsoft paid $12 million to use one of their songs (the real total was "only" $3 million). The potentially risky campaign paid off immediately. Windows 95 would sell 40 million copies in the first year after being released, plus Microsoft was able to sell its applications—like MS Word—that were optimized for the operating system.[20] This was an exceptionally lucrative bet for Microsoft and was a central theme of the trial that began in 1998.

1996—GATES FEARING FAILURE

Customers tell me they worry that Microsoft, by definition the only source for Microsoft operating system software, could raise prices of slow down or even stop innovation. But if we did, we wouldn't be able to sell our new versions. Existing users wouldn't upgrade, and we wouldn't get any new users. Our revenue would fall, and other companies would come in and take our place. The positive-feedback mechanism helps challengers as well as the incumbent. A leader can't rest on its laurels because there's always a competitor coming up from behind.[21]

1997—GATES VIEWING WINDOWS AS THE ONLY OPTION

Gates was worried that Sun was becoming a competitive threat with Java, and was having a meeting with developers who were asked to test coding an application for the Internet instead of writing the code to operate within Windows. A team leader who was speaking for the Internet team's attempt started his presentation and encountered Gates's temper before leaving the very first slide, as Windows had yet to be mentioned: "Why don't you just give up your options and join the Peace Corps?" Mr. Gates is said to have thundered. "Hasn't anybody here ever heard of Windows? Windows is what this company is about!"[22]

This was a little harsh for Gates, who is known for frequently being abrasive in meetings. In fact, there's one phrase a presentation can elicit from Gates that is described as proudly adopted by the recipients: " 'That's the stupidest thing I've ever heard,' and victims wear it as a badge of honor, bragging about it the way they do about getting a late-night E-mail from him."[23]

MICROSOFT'S APPLE INVESTMENT

August 6, 1997. While Bill Gates maintained a multiple-decade run as CEO of Microsoft, Steve Jobs had previously been ousted from the company he had cofounded. Jobs had been completely detached from Apple for more than a decade (1985 until 1996), when Apple acquired the second computer company Jobs founded, NeXT. Now Jobs was in-charge of Apple again, albeit as the Interim CEO, and the firm was in a difficult financial downturn.

In the lead-up to the Microsoft antitrust trial that would define the firm in the late 1990s, what occurred next would seem unthinkable to many. Microsoft made a cash investment in Apple at a time when Apple needed cash.[24]

And the symbolism of the event—Microsoft helping a struggling Apple after previous lawsuits from Apple, while Microsoft was already under judicial sanctions—was not lost on many observers, as Jobs was standing on stage and Gates was projected on a large movie screen above him. Not only did observers comment about the event, Jobs did as well. Rick Webb noted:

In 1997 in Boston I had the pleasure of witnessing in person what Steve Jobs called "my worst and stupidest staging event ever."

Onstage at Macworld Boston, Jobs announced his settle-ment of legal disputes and a partnership with Microsoft. And in a move eerily reminiscent of his landmark 1984 advertisement, Bill Gates' satellite-broadcast image filled the hall, a looming face looking every bit the overlord out of place. He was the Orwellian big brother we had come to despise. People booed as he spoke. In the end, the deal was probably a good thing, but the symbolism was catastrophic.[25]

The 1984 advertisement referenced was shown during the Super Bowl in 1984. The ad was a takeoff of George Orwell's book of the same title, and the symbolism was that the Mac—to be released that week as a project of Steve Jobs—would be a form of revolution. Given the more recent history between Apple and Microsoft, the Apple fans at Macworld Boston booed Bill Gates, even as Gates was announcing the provision of software and technology resources for Apple, as well as

In a scene viewed as reminiscent of Apple's 1984 ad, Bill Gates is projected over Apple CEO Steve Jobs as Microsoft announces a financial investment and technical assistance that helped save Apple from failure. (AP Photo/Julia Malakie)

a non-voting investment of $150 million in company stock to ease the company's financial pain:

- Microsoft will develop and ship future versions of its popular Microsoft Office productivity suite, Internet Explorer and other Microsoft tools for the Mac platform.
- Apple will bundle the Microsoft Internet Explorer browser with the Mac OS, making it the default browser in future operating system software releases.
- The companies agreed to a broad patent cross-licensing agreement. It paves the way for the two companies to work more closely on leading-edge technologies for the Mac platform.
- Apple and Microsoft plan to collaborate on technology to ensure compatibility between their respective Virtual Machines for Java and other programming languages.

- To further support its relationship with Apple, Microsoft will invest $150 million in non-voting Apple stock.[26]

Former partner Microsoft stepped in with a cash infusion of $150 million to help Apple at a point when bankruptcy was seen as a real possibility for Apple. While all of the actions taken by Microsoft could be easily seen as increasing the potential market for Microsoft products, others felt that the effort to invest in Apple was directly influenced by the antitrust lawsuits the company was defending at the time. And the "non-voting" component of the stock would likely be designed to suggest no power at all over a company that made similar products. The joint video announcement—made by Steve Jobs and Bill Gates—shows a cooperative arrangement with a competitor to the Windows operating system rather than direct attempts to harm a competitor. This announcement was made just two months before the U.S. government filed the second, more commonly known federal antitrust suit against Microsoft, and Gates had to defend his firm from multiple angles at the next Microsoft shareholder meeting.

FLYING AS THE RICHEST MAN IN THE WORLD

Although Gates had been ranked for many years as the richest man in the world, he flew commercial airlines until 1997. Not one to be ostentatious in public, he did not even fly in business or first class, just a standard seat in economy/coach. "His preference on long trips was to throw a blanket over his head and sleep." Given increasing demands in his travel schedule, Gates bought a Bombardier Challenger 604 private jet in October 1997 for $21 million, which he decided to use for business and personal purposes. Gates did not believe it was appropriate to have Microsoft pay for the aircraft, so the plane purchase was a personal one.[27]

BILL GATES AT THE 1997 SHAREHOLDER MEETING

The date was November 14, 1997. Microsoft was holding the company's annual shareholder meeting, and the government had already filed the contempt motion, alleging that the company had violated a settlement document signed in 1995. And Ralph Nader had conveniently scheduled an anti-Microsoft conference across the country for the same date. In addition to the items that excite Gates about technology, he also had to address threats to the business.

He noted how quickly the Internet moves, and that each year would see radical changes. He talked about the simplicity—or lack thereof—in 1997, where "Using a personal computer today is still more frustrating, still more complicated than we'd like it to be. And people are trying to do more and more with their personal computers."[28]

He talked about the *Digital Nervous System*, a metaphor he created to talk about how technology gets used now that the Internet was prevalent. And the Digital Nervous System would become far more widely known in 1999, as that was the year Gates published a best-selling book about the topic (*Business @ The Speed of Thought: Using a Digital Nervous System*). To the Microsoft shareholders present in 1997, he offered this:

It's a term I came up with to describe the idea that every business in this Information Age has to think of how they best use personal computers connected to the Internet to change the way that information flows inside their company, the way the (sic) deal with standard process like sales planning and employee management, the way they deal with surprises like a project being delayed or a competitor coming out with something that's particularly strong.

Of the events occurring outside Microsoft, he talked about how three of the other largest companies—IBM, Oracle, and Sun—were working together against his company's initiatives. He felt that Nader's conference was funded by competitors to hurt Microsoft in the court of public opinion, and he wanted to clarify how the company had decided to move toward including browser technology into Windows:

Our decision to put browser technology into the operating system actually predates the founding of Netscape. It was not a decision that was made based on some view of competitive dynamics. It was simply a natural progression of putting integrated features into our operating system. And our right to continue to do these integrated features is irrespective of whether those capabilities have been available separately in advance.[29]

His declaration that the idea "predates the founding of Netscape" could be debated. In his book about the *Digital Nervous System*, Gates notes: "After the first (retreat), on April 6, 1994, I e-mailed my staff to say, 'We're going to make a big bet on the Internet.'"[30]

Mosaic Communications Corporation was founded on April 4, 1994, and was later renamed Netscape on November 14, 1994, because "Mosaic" was the name of the web-browser most of the staff had worked on previously at NCSA. While the Netscape timing is thus unclear, the staff Netscape hired from NCSA clearly pre-dated Microsoft's decision.

As a reminder of Gates's consistently high intensity he said the following concerning the Internet and shipping an operating system without a browser: "Any operating system without a browser is going to be f_____ out of business," he says. "Should we improve our product, or go out of business?"[31]

1998—OPPORTUNITIES LOST

Gates's firm control of the company's decision making led to many lost opportunities over time. An example was the creation of an e-book reader by a team of engineers. The team developing the product thought that the CEO would absolutely love the product, which would fill a need that became apparent a decade later. Yes, Microsoft engineers were presenting what was effectively a Kindle, nine years before that device was first introduced by Amazon in 2007. Gates dismissed the project because the e-book reader interface did not look like Windows.

> By 1998 a prototype of the revolutionary tool was ready to go. Thrilled with its success and anticipating accolades, the technology group sent the device to Bill Gates—who promptly gave it a thumbs-down. The e-book wasn't right for Microsoft, he declared.
>
> "He didn't like the user interface, because it didn't look like Windows," one programmer involved in the project recalled. But Windows would have been completely wrong for an e-book, team members agreed. The point was to have a book, and a book alone, appear on the full screen. Real books didn't have images from Microsoft Windows floating around; putting them into an electronic version would do nothing but undermine the consumer experience.[32]

INTELLECTUAL PROPERTY REVISITED, GLOBAL EDITION

Despite vigorously fighting to protect the intellectual property rights of Microsoft for more than two decades, Gates recognized that the world was changing rapidly. While computers and Internet usage were becoming much more prevalent in the United States and other industrialized nations, other regions still had opportunities for much more growth. Gates went on record as acknowledging that individuals and companies in those regions might be in the same scenario as the software industry of the 1970s and early 1980s in the United States, where widespread copying of software occurred frequently without direct financial benefit to the company that originally wrote the software. In the late 1990s, the success of Microsoft in many countries allowed Gates to make one really key rationalization: that the unauthorized copying of the company's software in some rapidly growing countries might help establish a standard, precisely as had occurred in the United States. And establishing a standard meant that more individuals and companies would be reliant upon Microsoft products in future years: "About three million computers get sold every year in China, but people don't pay for the software. Someday, they will, though. As long as they are going to steal it, we want them to steal ours. They'll get sort of addicted, and then we'll somehow figure out how to collect sometime in the next decade."[33]

Microsoft still continues to promote initiatives to protect intellectual property, domestically and abroad. The firm provides an introduction to intellectual property in its current Software Asset Management (SAM) initiative targeted toward businesses. The company speaks of the forms of intellectual property that cover intangible items like software (patents, copyrights, and trademarks) and that software is protected under copyright. As Gates had long argued, the company's document on SAM says intellectual property rights have to be strong enough to convince authors and inventors to create the item, while using the work of others in a limited way allows others to grow and expand knowledge (like the quotes used in this book). The World Trade Organization (WTO) oversees the Agreement on Trade Related Aspects of Intellectual Property Rights (TRIPS) that most countries in the world have now signed. Microsoft also talks about the risks to the firm that knowingly—or unknowingly—uses nongenuine software, including various forms of security breaches like malware and viruses that might be in the unlicensed versions. China signed the TRIPS agreement in 2001, in theory closing the storyline of Bill Gates seeking to protect Microsoft's intellectual property. Not only had he achieved a legal determination in the United States, but countries where he was previously willing to accept unlicensed software began to protect intellectual property on a global level.[34]

1998—A PATH AWAY FROM MICROSOFT VIA STEVE BALLMER

As Gates had already spent 23 years as CEO of Microsoft, he began to speak of a day when he would not be CEO. Even before the U.S. Department of Justice trial began against Microsoft, Gates provided a hint at his future in a Town Hall event at the University of Washington in mid-1998, noting:

> "I think probably a decade from now or so—even though I'll still be totally involved with Microsoft because it's my career—I will pick somebody else to be CEO." He went on to say: "Picking that next person is something I give a lot of thought to, but it's probably five years before I have to do something concrete about it. If there was a surprise, well, there's a contingency plan."[35]

Gates had only ever spoken of one person as being able to provide the ideas and feedback he needed after Allen was no longer involved with the firm. And that was Ballmer, although Ballmer had a few structural failings in the organization. While he was good for brainstorming with Gates and questioning how Gates allocated time to avoid overexertion, he was always the number-two staffer after Allen left. No matter what Ballmer believed, Gates was always the decision maker. Ballmer moving from his current role to an elevated one may—or may not—still require deferring to Gates's wishes.

> It's a phenomenal business partnership. I wouldn't enjoy my job like I do if it wasn't for how much fun Steve and I have brainstorming things. And with the company, everybody has understood

that we work very closely together and have a very common view of where we want to go. Externally, people tend to identify the company with one person.

I have Steve look at my calendar. It's a conversation we have at least 10 times a year: "I'm feeling overloaded again. I wonder if I'm spending my time the right way?" And so Steve will get my calendar and flip through it and say, "Did you really need to do this speech? Did you need to meet with these guys?"[36]

Steve had accepted that he wasn't going to get the visibility, the glory, and the final decision on anything. . . . And I was good at saying, Steve, do you want to say anything more [while making decisions]? But I had to make the final decision.[37]

Five years from the 1998 town hall event would put one at 2003, and ten years from 1998 would be 2008. Gates would relinquish the role of CEO less than two years later, in January 2000—before the final ruling was issued in the Microsoft antitrust case—and left full-time duties at Microsoft in 2008. In fact, Gates would ask Steve Ballmer to take over as CEO the next year (1999), although the transition occurred in 2000. And Gates still had the expected trouble managing a transition from the CEO role to chairman and chief software architect, although he had specifically requested that Ballmer become CEO:

He (Gates) asked me to become CEO in '99, and I said, "Do you really want me to be CEO? If you do, I'll do it. But don't ask me to be CEO if you really still want to be CEO." He says, "No, I still really want you to be CEO." And neither one of us really kind of knew what to do differently. So, he probably tried a little bit too hard to have nothing change, and I probably tried a little bit too hard to have everything change. That was just a transition that we had to go through.[38]

Chapter 5

WHY WAS MICROSOFT SO SUCCESSFUL WITH BILL GATES?

Gates and Microsoft benefited from many economic concepts. As the first group to produce BASIC for the Altair, the company benefitted from first-mover advantage—the early company had the programming language that was available with the first computer the average consumer would afford. Being first in a market segment is often beneficial, as it is hard for competing organizations to catch up unless the first-mover runs into financial or structural problems. And once Microsoft moved from programming languages and began to sell and develop operating systems, this first-mover advantage became very entrenched. While there can easily be multiple programming languages used on the same computer, most computers come with just a single default operating system (like Windows).

Starting with MS-DOS and IBM, MS-DOS benefitted from being the first-mover on IBM (and IBM-compatible) PCs. With versions of BASIC on almost every computer made from the late 1970s through the mid-1980s, Microsoft's software would somehow be associated with the devices that gathered the most market share. This was an inevitable conclusion. Later, the addition of Windows while simultaneously developing OS/2 for IBM meant that a computer using an Intel-based processor in an average home would be running an operating system developed by Microsoft. Microsoft would often have more than 90 percent of the market in operating systems for computers in the home.

Going a step past the first-mover advantage, Microsoft's products set standards by default. If there were no other commercially viable options for operating systems on early IBM computers, everyone purchased Microsoft's operating system. As we learned over time, Microsoft began to see there would be potential competition against the standard that had been set, which led to the era of "per-processor licenses" that resulted in the first legal consent decree. The consent decree was issued because Microsoft developed contracts that required computer manufacturers (OEMs, or Original Equipment Manufacturers) to purchase a license for a Microsoft operating system for every computer they built and sold—even the computers with other operating systems installed. Stopping Microsoft from defending its first-mover advantage in this way was initially seen as the most important part of the 1994–1995 settlement.

Once the winning platforms were decided, Microsoft was there. On top of the now-ubiquitous Microsoft operating systems were Microsoft applications used in many different settings. And as more individuals became familiar with Microsoft's Windows, the devices became more and more prevalent. In this form of virtuous cycle, additional users brought even more individuals into the Microsoft user base. This network effect is reinforcing to an extent; each new user creates more value than the previous; this happens with any form of connection. The adoption of the Internet was also a virtuous cycle that caught Gates a little off-guard.

As the developer of languages on many computers, operating systems on many computers, and later the developer of applications on the winning platforms, Microsoft helped secure the company's own success through path dependence. Once sufficiently far down a path—whether figuratively or literally—changing paths can become really difficult. If commercial and home users become exceptionally comfortable with Windows and Microsoft Office, there becomes little incentive to change to a different operating system and application. When file types are based upon a certain application or operating system, this also creates a disincentive to change; the files made before a change might not be compatible with a new system. This encourages users to continue to use the same system to minimize switching costs, where those costs involve both money and time.

Prahalad and Hamel (1990) wrote about the concept of core competences[1]—the part of companies that creates the substantive part of their competitive advantage. Without a long-term competitive advantage, Microsoft products could have very easily ceased to exist sometime between 1975 and today, as many other computer and software companies have. For Microsoft, the initial core competence was related to programming languages, then operating systems, and then operating systems plus applications, which we can see by going through a few steps:

1. Does Microsoft benefit from operating systems and applications across a wide array of devices? Yes, from home computers to servers to phones and video game consoles and various other forms of electronics. Skills learned in one setting can be applied to others.

2. Do the products made by the company benefit the user? If someone knows how to use Microsoft Windows and a set of applications on a single device, switching to another device or another version of Windows is usually a comparatively easy process.

3. Is Microsoft software hard to imitate? Yes, as there is a lot of computer code involved in Microsoft Windows and a competitor that copies parts of the computer program would be in violation of Microsoft's intellectual property. While there are alternative operating systems and thousands of other applications, the common ones used by the average consumer are produced by either Microsoft or Apple.

Developing software costs money. In the case of the earliest versions of BASIC, we know that Gates mentioned spending $40,000 in the *Open Letter to Hobbyists*—in 1975 terms—developing the software, although the limitations of computers of the day meant the software being developed was small. In fact, the first version of Altair BASIC was fewer than 4,000 characters due to computer chip limitations. Now, major software development efforts can cost hundreds of millions of dollars, and Microsoft was reported to have spent $300 million in advertising alone for Windows 95. In order to remain profitable, Microsoft had to:

1. Make products that consumers saw as worth the upgrade. As Bill Gates himself had suggested Microsoft was paid for "breakthroughs"—a consumer could indeed elect to use a 10-year-old computer without upgrading if he or she desired.

2. Sell enough of every new product/operating system to cover the cost of development and advertising. Just like with the original Altair BASIC, Microsoft had to sell enough copies of the software to make up the investment in developing software, advertising, and making copies to sell. This explained his anger at fewer than 10 percent of Altair users in the first year actually buying his product.

3. If the company never sells enough copies of the software to cover the cost of development, advertising, and packaging (or downloads), the product will lose money. And many Microsoft products have indeed been unprofitable over time. Since 1995, there have been Microsoft Bob, Windows Me, Windows CE, and other products users have likely forgotten, even if purchased.

4. Only after selling enough copies of the product to cover the cost of development, advertising, and the comparatively minor cost of packaging/delivering the new product could the company begin to *actually make money*. However, this "break-even point" is where software companies need to be in order to exist; each new copy of the software sold after that point is almost all profit—for example, an extra license for a $99 piece of software on a $3 packaged DVD is $96 in profit (and the company can gather more profit if the product is sold as a download). The marginal revenue far exceeds the marginal cost after selling the first copy of the software.

Profitable companies create value; in the case of Microsoft, all of the costs are more than sufficiently covered with revenue, although the early days of the firm saw a shortfall on revenue for the Altair BASIC. Value-added items can also be based upon how items are put together—for many users, a box of computer parts plus some software has little value, but the computer manufacturer who puts all of those components together creates value.

Microsoft followed a path of vertical integration. While the firm did begin with programming languages, there was a progression to operating systems, applications, and utilities. Everything except the physical components of the computer was developed and coordinated by Microsoft—and the company has made physical hardware—but that close integration between all of the software (like Windows 95 and Internet Explorer) did lead to the Microsoft antitrust trial.

There's one word Gates and Microsoft never wanted to hear from a government regulator. Actually, there were two: monopoly and antitrust, where the latter is how the government decides to handle monopolies. In the period from late 1997 through 2002, the Sherman Antitrust Act of 1890 would shape almost all media references to Microsoft, despite the release of popular products like Windows 98, Windows 2000, and Windows XP.

Chapter 6

MICROSOFT TRIAL

We've done some good work, but all of these products become obsolete so fast. . . . It will be some finite number of years, and I don't know the number—before our doom comes.[1]

When considering the Microsoft trial with the U.S. Department of Justice (DOJ), one has to be aware that the series of events extended far beyond a single trial. The events that led to the trial started years before, and the repercussions of the trial lasted years afterward. In fact, Microsoft—and Bill Gates—had multiple opportunities to completely avoid a trial, and the actions and words of Gates shaped the perceptions of the public and judge involved in the trial.

THE FIRST CONSENT DECREE

Microsoft had been under investigation in the early 1990s, leading the company to agree to a consent decree with the DOJ in 1994. What's a consent decree? It's a legally binding document between two different parties—in this case, the DOJ and Microsoft—that states the defendant (Microsoft) will no longer undertake certain actions that the DOJ found to be unacceptable under various competition laws. Consent decrees are a way for the two parties to make an agreement—once approved by a judge—that are intended to stop unwanted behaviors without a trial and usually without admitting that the defendant (in this case Microsoft) had actually engaged in wrongdoing. Effectively, the consent decree is a listing of items that won't be done in the future to ensure compliance with the law. If a consent decree is violated, the plaintiff (DOJ) could then start a new proceeding against Microsoft. The initial consent decree was not approved by the first judge assigned to the case (U.S. District Court judge Stanley Sporkin), so there was a delay of almost a year before the decree went into effect. "This antitrust thing will blow over," Mr. Gates said. "We haven't changed our business practices at all"—attributed to Bill Gates on July 11, 1995, admitted as evidence in later antitrust trial.[2]

The first consent decree against Microsoft was approved by U.S. District Court judge Thomas Penfield Jackson on August 21, 1995, running for a period of 6.5 years from that date. As noted in the *New York Times*, Judge Jackson was ready to bring the judicial review process to a quick end after Microsoft had been investigated for almost five years: "For his part, Judge Jackson made it clear yesterday that he intended to bring the extended period of judicial review to an abrupt close. 'This hearing will be short and sweet, ladies and gentlemen,' he said in opening the 20-minute session."[3]

Jackson had been a judge on the U.S. District Court for many years, and had presided over other high-profile cases. He was the judge who presided over the case and sentencing of former Washington, D.C. mayor Marion Barry to prison in a drug case, writing that Barry "has given aid, comfort and encouragement to the drug culture at large, and contributed to the anguish that illegal drugs have inflicted on this city in so many ways for so long."[4] This trait of not accepting misconduct in a no-nonsense manner will reappear, as Microsoft was not done with Judge Jackson's court.

As a firm, Microsoft's lawyers argued that the consent decree should have been back-dated to when Microsoft had—in fact—been willing to accept the decree as written before Judge Sporkin rejected the agreement. Judge Jackson denied the request, and Microsoft would be back in his courtroom well before the expiration of the consent decree. Lohr wrote prophetically:

> Antitrust experts agree that Microsoft cannot expect to be left alone by the Government, if only because of its size and clout. "The Justice Department has made it pretty clear that Microsoft will remain under scrutiny," said Charles F. Rule, a partner in Covington & Burling and a former head of the Justice Department's antitrust division.[5]

At the time of the first consent decree, observers believed the most important part was related to preventing Microsoft from charging a "per processor" license fee, where computer manufacturers would have to pay Microsoft, even for computers that did not even have Microsoft's software:

> In July 1994, Microsoft and the Justice Department reached a settlement. The main effect of the consent decree is to end Microsoft's practice of "per processor" license agreements in which personal computer makers agree to pay a licensing fee for each computer shipped with a particular model of microprocessor, even for machines not loaded with Microsoft's operating software. Rivals said this practice had chilled the market for competing software.[6]

The date of Judge Jackson's action was August 21, 1995. The consent decree that had been approved but tied up in legal review—after being accepted by Microsoft but rejected by Judge Sporkin—included the following clause:

> E. Microsoft shall not enter into any License Agreement [with an OEM] in which the terms of that agreement are expressly or impliedly conditioned upon:
>
> > (i) the licensing of any other Covered Product, Operating System Software product or other product (provided, however, that this provision in and of itself shall not be construed to prohibit Microsoft from developing integrated products).[7]

The Windows 95 operating system came out precisely three days later, on August 24, 1995. And that operating system had something called Internet Explorer, formerly code-named O'Hare, which had been listed in Gates's *The Internet Tidal Wave* memo as a product to convince customers to switch from Netscape. Remarkably, there was little concern whether the product as implemented would be an impermissible "Covered Product" or an allowed "Integrated Product" under the consent decree because observers believed this clause was of minor importance at the time, far less important than preventing Microsoft from charging per-processor on computers shipped without Microsoft products.

COMPETITION IN BETWEEN

Osterland (1996), in *The case against Microsoft*, described how industry analysts believed the competitors would attack Microsoft in an way that could not be stopped, and that the market, according to Roxanne Googin, wanted to see Netscape and Java attack Microsoft, although the initial result would be a form of confusion. She contemplated Microsoft and how the firm received recurring revenue, which was licensing products to businesses and making those new innovations described by Bill Gates that led consumers at home to upgrading their products when major new releases came out. "Microsoft might do okay on the Internet, but it's not their schtick," says Googin. "It threatens the base upon which their valuation depends, and upon which they get their recurring revenue streams."[8]

OCTOBER 20, 1997

In two years, the government had decided—after watching Microsoft require licenses for Internet Explorer 3.0 and prepare for Internet Explorer 4—that Internet Explorer just might not be integrated. October 20, 1997, was the day the U.S. government filed a contempt motion against Microsoft for alleged violations of the initial consent decree. And while observers had believed the most important part of the first consent decree was stopping Microsoft from charging vendors for Windows on computers shipped with other operating systems, that belief proved to be untrue.

Why would adding what was viewed as a web browser to a computer be seen as a major event? In the early days of the Internet era, high-speed Internet was rare. Microsoft, now keenly aware of the potential for the Internet to revolutionize computing, included Microsoft's Internet Explorer in all new copies of Windows that shipped. At the same time, the company required computer manufacturers (OEM's, for Original Equipment Manufacturers) to ship their version of Windows with no other web browsers included.

Today, this would seem to be a fairly easy item to resolve—a user could simply go online and rapidly download an alternative browser and remove Internet Explorer just like any other program. During 1997/1998, this was a little more challenging. With far slower Internet speeds in 1998, the options were instead what could be a lengthy download process or purchasing a copy of an alternative web browser at a store to install at home. In addition, there were no published means of removing Internet Explorer that had been created by Microsoft (although computer scientists had figured out how to do so). Add the allegation that Microsoft altered the Windows operating system to favor the use of Internet Explorer, and the company was sued by the U.S. government and 20 states under the Sherman Antitrust Act of 1890,

Bill Gates and Steve Ballmer after the April 2000 ruling of U.S. District Court Judge Thomas Penfield Jackson that Microsoft was an unallowed monopoly. (AP Photo/Microsoft, Jeff Christensen)

specifically for chilling competition after violating the consent decree. However, testimony in the trial would show actions by Microsoft that could have reasonably harmed far more firms than Netscape.

Microsoft's product was included in Windows for free, at a time when competitors often charged for web browsers. Some of the more condemning statements suggested that Microsoft was intentionally trying to eliminate competitor Netscape—a for-profit firm—by offering a free version that closely mirrored the functions of Netscape Navigator.

IS INTERNET EXPLORER AN INTEGRATED COMPONENT?

In the build-up to the DOJ case against Microsoft, Joe Belfiore, group program manager for Windows User Interface, wrote a document "Internet Standards and Operating Systems—Why Integration Makes Sense," published in 1998. In that document, he explains what the code-name O'Hare really meant in Gates's *Internet Tidal Wave* memo.

> From the very outset, Microsoft intended Windows 95 to support the broadest possible range of networks, including the Internet. That is why the development of Windows 95, code-named "Chicago," included work on a variety of Internet-related technologies, code-named "O'Hare"—a point of departure to distant places from Chicago. These technologies were later referred to by the name "Internet Explorer," and Internet Explorer 1.0 was an integrated element of the first version of Windows 95 provided to computer manufacturers, 2½ years ago.[9]

So "O'Hare" (named after Chicago's largest airport) became the very first version of Internet Explorer, taking users far away from Chicago (Windows 95) while still in Chicago (Windows 95). Belfiore went on to talk about Internet Explorer as really serving two different roles:

> You may regard "Internet Explorer" as just a web browser application, but that would be quite an inaccurate way to think of it. In fact, "Internet Explorer" describes two things:
>
> 1. A set of platform technologies that any software vendor can use to make their application support Internet standards.

2. A user-interface that any consumer can use to view web-sites on the Internet or any other internet-standards-based network.

The first of these two things—the platform technologies—work just like the support for toolbars that Microsoft made a native part of Windows that anyone could use. Instead of requiring every separate software developer to assign a team of people the task of implementing computer code for handling Internet standards, Microsoft has written the code once and made it possible for anyone to use it. . . . That is a huge efficiency and enables software developers to focus their energies on adding attractive new features to their products rather than focusing on the low-level plumbing required to handle Internet standards.[10]

The question that could be asked from this statement would be whether the technology really "can" be used or "must" be used to connect to the Internet. If the answer was that all products, including other products issued by Microsoft, *must* use those platform technologies to connect to the Internet, a claim that the *platform technology* was truly an integrated one would be easier to make. If other software vendors had the option of using those technologies and the Windows operating system could connect to the Internet without Internet Explorer, then the product would not be seen as integrated (and thus against the consent decree). The ability to run Windows without Internet Explorer became a major issue in the trial, and Belfiore was called to testify.

The declaration that setting a standard makes life easier for other programmers likely sounds familiar; Bill Gates had made a quote in 1977 that the industry might have benefitted from a single operating system that everyone else works from. And if this description of Windows Explorer being a web browser *plus* a platform that companies could use (not required to use) to make their software support the Internet seems to suggest that Internet Explorer was not absolutely essential to run Windows, one might also be correct.

HEADED TO TRIAL

As the government's contempt order was winding toward a trial in Judge Jackson's courtroom, Gates was speaking publicly to defend his

firm and the importance of providing access to the Internet. He es-
poused that the government was claiming that Microsoft's products
were too capable, that successful businesses are often the target of comments from naysayers, and that the Internet cannot be controlled or
dominated by any entity (including Microsoft). Gates also suggested
that Microsoft had added the capability of connecting to the Internet
as a convenience to software developers (as Belfiore similarly claimed):

> Part of the PC dynamic is that instead of asking software devel-
> opers to duplicate one another's work, we take anything that's
> typical in all those applications and put those features in Win-
> dows. So for things like connecting to the Internet, instead of
> everybody having to do that themselves, we put that in. That's
> been the evolution—graphical user interfaces came in, hard-disk
> support, networking support, now Internet support, including the
> browser.[11]

DETOUR TO THE SENATE JUDICIARY COMMITTEE

Gates was called to speak before the Senate Judiciary Committee on
March 3, 1998. At that time, the suggestion that he was not always
forthcoming when questioned about Microsoft's behavior began to
become national news. The *Congressional Record* detailed a particular
exchange between Senator Orrin Hatch (the chairperson of the Senate
Judiciary Committee at the time) and Bill Gates, when Hatch followed
up an existing ambiguity by asking a version of a yes/no question five
times in an attempt to draw an answer from Gates about his firm's behavior against Netscape.

Hatch: Mr. Gates, you have been somewhat hard to nail down
on a very specific question, and I would appreciate just
a yes or no, if you can. Do you put any limitation on
content providers that limit them . . . for advertising or
promoting Netscape? Yes or no, if you can.

Gates: Every Internet content provider that has a business
relationship with Microsoft is free to develop content
that uses competitors' platforms and standards.

Hatch: But my question is do you put any limitations on content providers that limit them . . . for doing any advertising or promoting Netscape?

Gates: Well, understand, there are more people in the Netscape channel guide than there are on the Microsoft channel guide.

Hatch: How about Microsoft: Do they put limitations or restrictions on people from advertising and promoting Netscape?

Gates: I am not aware of any limitation that prevents them from doing content that promotes Netscape.

Hatch: Do you use your exclusive arrangements with the companies—do you use that as leverage to stop them from advertising or promoting Netscape?

Gates: I don't—we don't—. . .

Hatch: Does Microsoft then limit—place and limit on any content providers that limits them . . . for advertising or promoting Netscape or any other competitor?

Gates: I said earlier that on the pages that you link to through the channel guide—that on those pages you don't promote the competitive product, but that is a unique URL. You are free to promote their content in quite a variety of ways, but not off the specific page that we link to.[12]

HOW DID THIS HAPPEN?

When the DOJ filed a motion to declare Microsoft in contempt of the first consent decree, the reasoning was that Windows and Internet Explorer were both covered products under the consent decree, a combination that would not be allowed. Microsoft would argue that Internet Explorer was integrated into Windows, so the product was allowed within the scope of the consent decree. Once the investigation reopened, the U.S. government and U.S. states suing Microsoft were able to look into many more issues than just the connection between Windows and Internet Explorer; in fact, the investigation looked into behaviors toward competitors that would also be anticompetitive or violate the initial consent decree in other ways.

Operating systems—then and now—of course already had a large number of included tools, so a question revolves around what counts as integrated and what does not. Given the progression from programming languages to operating systems to applications to utilities as software a computer would frequently use, Windows would be an operating system, Microsoft Office is an application that runs on the operating system, and there were already dozens of nice little add-on utilities like calculators, fax capability, and MS Paint, which themselves could preclude competitors. Clearly, Microsoft had the ability to add some features and functionality to Windows without running afoul of the consent decree.

AUGUST 27, 1998: THE FIRST DAY OF THE GATES DEPOSITION

Gates gave his deposition not in a courtroom or the office of attorneys but in a boardroom at Microsoft headquarters, beginning August 27, 1998. Kawamoto quoted a source familiar with the deposition as saying he was "evasive and nonresponsive" to the questions asked on day one, and "the source said that when Gates was asked to verify a quote attributed to him in a published article, he said he would have to view the transcript of the interview to see its full context before commenting." The first day of the deposition lasted nine hours, so there were many questions of Gates from the states and the DOJ. And the media was already reporting—before the case began—that Gates was not coming across as a sympathetic character.[13]

In Gates's deposition (used in the Microsoft trial), he was challenged by many of the DOJ attorneys on competitive issues and came across as being disconnected from the actions of the firm of which he was the CEO, despite two decades of statements that Gates was excessively involved with the firm. On a critical case that could shape the future of the firm, Gates asserted that he had never read the DOJ filing or been given a summary of the case against Microsoft:

Q: Now, have you ever read the complaint in this case?
A: No.

Q: Have you ever received a summary of the complaint in this case?

A: I wouldn't say I've received a summary, no. I've talked to my lawyers about the case but not really the complaint.

On a June 23, 1996, e-mail to internal staff at Microsoft.

Q: In the second paragraph you say, "I have 2 key goals in investing in the Apple relationship 1) Maintain our applications share on the platform and 2) See if we can get them to embrace Internet Explorer in some way." Do you see that?

A: Yeah.

In 1997, when Apple and Microsoft had launched a partnership at MacWorld Boston, there was an e-mail involving Gates that noted that the threat of cancelling the MacOffice 97 project would harm Apple immediately, and thus would be the strongest bargaining point.

Q: Now, let me direct your attention to the second item on the first page of this exhibit. And this purports to be an e-mail from Mr. Waldman to you dated June 27, 1997; is that correct, sir?

A: The second one, uh-huh.

Q: You have to answer audibly yes or no, Mr. Gates.

A: Yes, the second one.

Q: Now, in the second paragraph of this e-mail to you, the second sentence reads, "The threat to cancel Mac Office 97 is certainly the strongest bargaining point we have, as doing so will do a great deal of harm to Apple immediately." Do you see that, sir?

A: Uh-huh.

Q: Do you recall receiving this e-mail in June of 1997?

A: Not specifically.

Q: Do you have any doubt that you received this e-mail in June of 1997?

A: No.

Post-agreement with Apple, there was a communication about using Apple to undermine both Sun and Netscape, in a three-line message written by Bill Gates:

Q: So the subject is post-agreement with Apple, and the very first sentence is, "I want to get as much mileage as possible out of our browser and Java relationship here." Second sentence says, "In other words, a real advantage against Sun and Netscape." Third line says, "Who should Avie be working with? Do we have a clear plan on what we want Apple to do to undermine Sun?" Now, do you have any doubt that when you talk about, "I want to get as much mileage as possible out of our browser and Java relationship here," you're talking about Apple?

A: That's what it appears.

Further information includes moving Netscape out of the market segment that would include Windows 95, including an e-mail that Gates had apparently sent to have Apple interfere in Sun's business.

Q: The e-mail goes on to list working goals which are:

"1. Launch STT, our electronic payment protocol. Get STT presence on the Internet.
2. Move Netscape out of the Win32 Internet client area.
3. Avoid cold or hot war with Netscape. Keep them from sabotaging our platform evolution."

Do you understand the reference to Win32 Internet client to be a reference to Windows 95?

A: No

Q: Well, let me show you a document and try to probe what you mean by being involved. Let me give you a copy of a document that has been previously marked as Government Exhibit 265. A portion of this document is an e-mail message from you to Paul Maritz and others and the portion I'm particularly interested in, and you can read as much of the three-line e-mail as you wish, is the last sentence, which reads, "Do we have a clear plan on what we want Apple to do to undermine Sun?" Did you send this e-mail, Mr. Gates, on or about August 8, 1997?

A: I don't remember sending it.

Q: Do you have any doubt that you sent it?

A: No. It appears to be an e-mail I sent.

When copied on an e-mail that Microsoft should work to convince Apple to materially disadvantage Netscape, Gates admits he did not order his staff to stop attempts to harm the firm.

Q: Did you ever say to Mr. Bradford in words or substance in February of 1998 or thereafter, "Mr. Bradford, you've got it wrong, we're not out to significantly or materially disadvantage Netscape through Apple"?

A: No.

Q: Did you ever tell Mr. Bradford or anyone else in February, 1998 or thereafter, that they should not be trying to get Apple to do things that would significantly or materially disadvantage Netscape?

A: No.

GATES'S TESTIMONY IN THE TRIAL

One of the more surprising components of the highly publicized Microsoft trial was that Bill Gates was the single-most important figure but never actually testified in the trial. He was never called as a witness by Microsoft's legal team, and the government could not compel him to testify unless he was testified in Microsoft's defense. His involvement in the trial was solely based upon his deposition taken by the various lawyers in August 1998, which was admitted into the court record over a series of days.

Gates's recorded deposition was apparently considered to be epically beneficial to the government's case against Microsoft. Components of the videotaped deposition made frequent appearances in court. In fact, while dozens of other individuals were deposed and had parts of their depositions aired in court on one or two days, Gates's videotaped deposition made many appearances, over eight different days from early November 1998 through January 1999.

There was video of Gates played on November 2, 9, 16, and 17; December 2 and 15; and again on January 5. And procedurally, the whole deposition was admitted into the court record on January 13, 1999.[14] How bad did these appearances seem to be in real time in Judge Jackson's courtroom? As reported in late 1998:

> By most measures, the flesh-and-blood Gates has come off far less admirably in his videotaped performance at his company's antitrust trial. He squirms and hedges. He argues with prosecutors over the definition of commonly used words, including "we" and "compete." Early rounds of his deposition show him offering obfuscatory answers and saying "I don't recall" so many times that even the presiding judge had to chuckle. Worse, many of the technology chief's denials and pleas of ignorance have been directly refuted by prosecutors with snippets of E-mail Gates both sent and received. And it's far from over: The government has taped more than 20 hours of testimony from Gates, which it plans to play in snatches as the trial unwinds over the next two months.[15]

The case would seem to be going poorly for Microsoft if the judge was laughing at the responses he was hearing from Bill Gates. The case would seem to be going exceptionally poorly if the judge had *visible* reactions to the statements made by Microsoft's lawyers. "Reporters noted that Judge Jackson rolled his eyes or scowled at statements by Microsoft's attorneys and laughed during videotaped testimony by company cofounder Bill Gates."[16]

The firm claimed that Internet Explorer was so integrated into the Windows 98 product that the functionality could not be removed without slowing down Windows but the government had developed a program that was claimed—and reported by the press—as removing Internet Explorer and not hurting the performance of Windows 98. Microsoft vice president James Allchin was on the stand when Microsoft decided to show a video of the performance of the computers. Unfortunately, someone at the company had filmed the wrong computers, and the U.S. government's lead lawyer—David Boies—pounced on Allchin's and Microsoft's credibility, not once but twice. And even when Allchin repeated the demonstration for the court, the press did not report the results that favored Microsoft's claim.

> The video flap, he says slowly, "was the most humiliating moment of my professional life." He's lost sleep over it. He's tried to imagine how he could have handled things differently. He wishes he'd taken more control over the making of the video. "Having my integrity questioned was super, super hard for me," he says. Which is not to say he's making excuses for what happened. "It was our own fault," he tells me sorrowfully.[17]

Microsoft had a difficult case to make and Judge Jackson had a lot of evidence to analyze once the case was rested. Gates was, in a conversation with an author writing a book about the trial, exceptionally pragmatic in stating: "No matter what the outcome, the lawsuit is a bad thing. The costs to the company and the taxpayers have been huge. The last thing any company wants is to be sued by the government."[18]

BETWEEN THE TRIAL CLOSING AND JUDGMENT

In the time between the trial closing and the issuance of the Statement of Fact in the Microsoft case, Gates continued to be quoted in various venues.

> When somebody's successful, people leap to simple explanations that might make sense. So you get these myths. People love to have any little story. Yes, I'm intense. I'm energetic. I like to understand what our market position is. But then it gets turned into this—the ultracompetitor. It's somewhat dehumanizing. I read that and say, I don't know that guy.[19]
>
> You basically have to convince the other guys not to spend enough money to compete with us, to keep just making it harder and harder, move the terms up, we just keep raising the bar, and eventually maybe one of them will try to do stuff with us. But a lot of them will just say "Forget It."[20]

LEAKED MICROSOFT MEMO AFTER
THE RECESS OF THE TRIAL

In the first of two times a Microsoft lawyer was noted by name in the media in relation to the antitrust trial, a memo written on March 3, 1999, was leaked to a member of the press—indirectly—the next week. In that memo, David Heiner wrote that the government's had proven no charges against Microsoft, the case against Microsoft was harming consumers, and that all the government had done was create a "lot of noise around various random incidents or pieces of E-mail."[21] Judge Jackson would disagree with Mr. Heiner.

THE FINDINGS OF FACT

Judge Thomas Penfield Jackson's Findings of Fact were issued on November 5, 1999. While readily available online in both html and PDF format today, the initial findings were not posted online. In fact, reading the findings of fact took a while for Microsoft staff, as Judge Jackson used a competitor to Microsoft's Word to create the electronic file (probably the earliest clear indicator of his judgment in the case). In his findings of fact, he does declare Microsoft to be a monopoly that used monopoly power, in violation of the Sherman Antitrust Act of 1890.

> With Jackson's decisive ruling on the facts, Microsoft appeared to be buried. It had dug itself deeper into its hole, a hole started with its take-no-prisoners corporate culture, a hole that deepened when it refused to alter its behavior even though it had signed a 1994 consent decree to do so, a hole it then dug still deeper when it openly distained Washington and government regulators or treated Judge Jackson as if he was a dim-witted Luddite when he ruled in December 1997 that Microsoft untie its browser from Windows 95, a hole it expanded when Gates did not reach a negotiated settlement with Justice in May 1998, and a hole it transformed into a cavern when a belligerent Gates was deposed.[22]

> 33. Microsoft enjoys so much power in the market for Intel-compatible PC operating systems that if it wished to exercise this power solely in terms of price, it could charge a price for Windows substantially above that which could be charged in a competitive

market. Moreover, it could do so for a significant period of time without losing an unacceptable amount of business to competitors. In other words, Microsoft enjoys monopoly power in the relevant market.[23]

On this, there was little disagreement; for Intel-compatible PCs, Microsoft was the primary operating system on the primary platform. There were other nascent options like Linux (a free, open-source program similar to Unix) available for PCs and servers but Microsoft was the sole option for most users on PCs, as Mac OS was—and remains—on the Mac, with periodic upgrades. However, the market scope of the PC was much greater.

> 34. Viewed together, three main facts indicate that Microsoft enjoys monopoly power. First, Microsoft's share of the market for Intel-compatible PC operating systems is extremely large and stable. Second, Microsoft's dominant market share is protected by a high barrier to entry. Third, and largely as a result of that barrier, Microsoft's customers lack a commercially viable alternative to Windows.[24]

Microsoft's share was indeed large, and the cost to develop and promote a new operating system would create a barrier to entry. The question is "how high"? Could an organization have readily re-envisioned what an operating system was and released a product that grew rapidly? We have recent evidence from the introduction of Google Chromebooks that a new entrant to the market can rapidly grow market share, using partnerships with firms that also produce Windows netbooks.

> 408. The debut of Internet Explorer and its rapid improvement gave Netscape an incentive to improve Navigator's quality at a competitive rate. The inclusion of Internet Explorer with Windows at no separate charge increased general familiarity with the Internet and reduced the cost to the public of gaining access to it, at least in part because it compelled Netscape to stop charging for Navigator. These actions thus contributed to improving the quality of Web browsing software, lowering its cost, and increasing its availability, thereby benefitting consumers.[25]

Here, Judge Jackson says that Internet Explorer and the active competition between Microsoft and Netscape was actually beneficial to consumers and made the cost cheaper and more accessible. This is not a normal clause to write in a ruling that a company is a monopoly. And Netscape was still a for-profit company that was purchased by AOL the year before, using the browser to direct customers to their websites and portals. Unlike consumers, business users still paid for Netscape Navigator and AOL had stressed that despite owning Netscape, partnering with Microsoft was still a strategic priority for the firm.

Microsoft stated there were 12,000 software firms, Netscape distributed 160 million copies the past year, and Netscape was on 40 percent of all Windows 98 machines. Many users were finding competition in a market that had been deemed to be a monopoly in these findings.[26]

> 409. To the detriment of consumers, however, Microsoft has done much more than develop innovative browsing software of commendable quality and offer it bundled with Windows at no additional charge. As has been shown, Microsoft also engaged in a concerted series of actions designed to protect the applications barrier to entry, and hence its monopoly power, from a variety of middleware threats, including Netscape's Web browser and Sun's implementation of Java. Many of these actions have harmed consumers in ways that are immediate and easily discernible. They have also caused less direct, but nevertheless serious and far-reaching, consumer harm by distorting competition.[27]

This part of the findings was indeed a problem for Microsoft, as there was ample evidence that the company did try to restrict those firms in the market, often by using leverage with other firms (like Apple).

> By constraining the freedom of OEMs to implement certain software programs in the Windows boot sequence, Microsoft foreclosed an opportunity for OEMs to make Windows PC systems less confusing and more user-friendly, as consumers desired. By taking the actions listed above, and by enticing firms into exclusivity arrangements with valuable inducements that only Microsoft could offer and that the firms reasonably believed they could

not do without, Microsoft forced those consumers who otherwise would have elected Navigator as their browser to either pay a substantial price (in the forms of downloading, installation, confusion, degraded system performance, and diminished memory capacity) or content themselves with Internet Explorer.[28]

Jackson determined that Microsoft had written contracts that would not allow the computer manufacturers to have other software boot automatically with Windows, yet Internet Explorer was included by default. He noted that consumers could still choose Netscape's Navigator but would pay some form of price as a result (although not a monetary cost).

412. Most harmful of all is the message that Microsoft's actions have conveyed to every enterprise with the potential to innovate in the computer industry. Through its conduct toward Netscape, IBM, Compaq, Intel, and others, Microsoft has demonstrated that it will use its prodigious market power and immense profits to harm any firm that insists on pursuing initiatives that could intensify competition against one of Microsoft's core products. Microsoft's past success in hurting such companies and stifling innovation deters investment in technologies and businesses that exhibit the potential to threaten Microsoft. The ultimate result is that some innovations that would truly benefit consumers never occur for the sole reason that they do not coincide with Microsoft's self-interest.[29]

Judge Jackson is very clear on his thoughts in this final statement. Microsoft's market power did allow for discussions about how to react to competitors, often in a way that would increase costs and/or limit markets. A question was whether Microsoft truly used the immense profits to harm other firms. There were immense profits that could have been used (that would then be "expenses," in accounting terms), but did Microsoft intentionally decrease profitability to harm other competitors? Or did Bill Gates see positions in the computer industry as so tenuous that he had to compete in a way that assumed Microsoft could fail overnight. Over the years, he made many statements that Microsoft would one day end, and that no company had an assured spot in the industry.

GATES'S RESPONSE TO THE FINDINGS OF FACT

Gates issued a response to the findings of fact as issued by Judge Jackson, and noted that the findings of fact would not be the last step in the legal process, as Microsoft did not agree with the ruling. Among the components of the statement, Gates mentioned "built-in support for the Internet" but without referring to the previous consent decree. The previous consent decree had provided limits in what could be added in current—and future—Windows operating systems. He stressed that the court did recognize that customers benefited from Microsoft's initial foray into the Internet, that Microsoft would be pursuing the case, and closed with the assertion that Microsoft was simply seeking to provide more resources for consumers.

> The court's findings do acknowledge that Microsoft's actions accelerated the development of the Internet, reduced the cost to consumers and improved the quality of Web-browsing software.
>
> Microsoft competes vigorously and fairly. Microsoft is committed to resolving this case in a fair and a factual manner, while ensuring that the principles of consumer benefits and innovation are protected.
>
> The lawsuit is fundamentally about one question: Can a successful American company continue to improve its products for the benefit of consumers? That is precisely what Microsoft did by developing new versions of the Windows operating system with built-in support for the Internet.[30]

WORLD WAR 3.0

David Boies, after the trial, noted the following to the author of *World War 3.0*:

> That deposition played a very important role in what happened at the trial. At the end of the day, when the findings are written, they can't be written without referring to the Gates deposition. That deposition did several things. First, it effectively knocked Gates out as a witness. . . . This deposition framed the trial. It made every Microsoft witness much more subject to a credibility test.
>
> Gates deposition effectively precluded Microsoft from coming up with a benign explanation for their behavior because Gates was the

central decision maker, and Gates was unable to come up with the explanations.[31]

An astute litigator, Boies was indeed correct. The lawyers for Microsoft would have difficulty having Gates, the CEO, testify in the trial given the chain of e-mails provided and the content of the deposition. Right or wrong, any testimony that concurred with—or conflicted—the content of the deposition would have harmed Microsoft.

MICROSOFT RENEWED ATTACK—MAY 22, 2000

In the period before the ruling, Microsoft asked that earlier court documents—from the consent decree five years earlier—be used in the new case to argue against breaking up the company. Those documents were issued by the government and talked about how a breakup of Microsoft would harm the economy and consumers.

> "Microsoft did a whole bunch more things wrong after the consent decree," said Robert Litan, vice president and director of economic studies at the Brookings Institution. Litan, who was a deputy assistant attorney general between 1993 and 1995, helped negotiate the 1995 consent decree in the earlier case against Microsoft. "A breakup is not as preposterous today as it was back then."[32]

Bill Gates giving his ill-fated testimony before the Senate Judiciary Committee, in March, 1998. (AP Photo)

However, in May 2000, the article further noted: "Securities analysts and some antitrust experts say the odds that Microsoft will eventually be split in two are remote. Even if Judge Jackson were to order such a split, he is very likely to be reversed on appeal." Effectively, the experts did not believe that Microsoft would ever be split even if Judge Jackson made a ruling that the best regulatory option would be splitting Microsoft into two firms; this bit of light foreshadowing tells us what happens next.[33]

The order to break apart Microsoft was issued by Judge Thomas Penfield Jackson on June 7, 2000. Appeals of this verdict were certain, as is the case of most highly contested trials. However, the future of Microsoft seemed a little dimmer at the time. The judge explicitly called for:

> the separation of the Operating Systems Business from the Applications Business, and the transfer of the assets of one of them (the "Separated Business") to a separate entity along with (a) all personnel, systems, and other tangible and intangible assets (including Intellectual Property) used to develop, produce, distribute, market, promote, sell, license and support the products and services of the Separated Business, and (b) such other assets as are necessary to operate the Separated Business as an independent and economically viable entity.[34]

When reading the judgment, one can discern that Judge Jackson defined the "operating system business" first (although that definition is much later in the document), then made the "applications business" everything not included in the operating system business. And by everything else, he meant everything else.

> "Operating Systems Business" means the development, licensing, promotion, and support of Operating System Products for computing devices including but not limited to (i) Personal Computers, (ii) other computers based on Intel x86 or competitive microprocessors, such as servers, (iii) handheld devices such as personal digital assistants and cellular telephones, and (iv) television set-top boxes.

"Applications Business" means all businesses carried on by Microsoft Corporation on the effective date of this Final Judgment except the Operating Systems Business. Applications Business includes but is not limited to the development, licensing, promotion, and support of client and server applications and Middleware (*e.g.*, Office, BackOffice, Internet Information Server, SQL Server, etc.), Internet Explorer, Mobile Explorer and other web browsers, Streaming Audio and Video client and server software, transaction server software, SNA server software, indexing server software, XML servers and parsers, Microsoft Management Server, Java virtual machines, Frontpage Express (and other web authoring tools), Outlook Express (and other e-mail clients), Media player, voice recognition software, Net Meeting (and other collaboration software), developer tools, hardware, MSN, MSNBC, Slate, Expedia, and all investments owned by Microsoft in partners or joint venturers, or in ISVs, IHVs, OEMs or other distributors, developers, and promoters of Microsoft products, or in other information technology or communications businesses.[35]

In the accompanying Memorandum and Order, Jackson stated that Microsoft lawyers knew all along that breaking up the company was possible, that Microsoft had never conceded to any violations, the company's conduct had not changed, and that Microsoft had been untrustworthy in the past. While stating that the structural division was required, Jackson noted "Microsoft as it is presently organized and led is unwilling to accept the notion that it broke the law or accede to an order amending its conduct."[36]

Jackson was prescient, noting in closing that the appeal of the breakup order would return to his courtroom and that the order to break up the company did not need to happen. Not *if* the ruling were to be appealed by Microsoft, but that the case *would* come back after appeal: "The final judgment proposed by plaintiffs is perhaps more radical than might have resulted had mediation been successful and terminated in a consent decree. . . . And, of course, the Court will retain jurisdiction following appeal, and can modify the judgment as necessary in

accordance with instructions from an appellate court or to accommodate conditions changed with the passage of time."[37]

Jackson knew that a settlement would not have resulted in a break-
up order, and that his break-up order was guaranteed to be appealed.
And although Gates was no longer CEO, he remained chairman of
Microsoft.

"This is the beginning of a new chapter in this case," Microsoft
Chairman Bill Gates said in a video statement. "We will be ap-
pealing this decision, and we have a very strong case on appeal.
This ruling is inconsistent with the past decisions by the appeals
court, with fundamental fairness and with the reality of the marketplace."[38]

BACKDROP IN CASE

Stephen, in *New Statesman,* described the impact of the ruling immediately on Microsoft. At the moment of the decision, Gates theo-
retically lost 15 percent of his total net worth as measured by external
entities. This ruling was a sizable blow to Gates, to Microsoft, and
the ability to operate the firm as had been done in the past. Stephen
noted his belief the success of Gates was not simply based upon his
technological capability but the technological capability paired with
he described as the "ruthlessness of a Murdoch," referring to Rupert
Murdoch, simultaneously suggesting that the combination of those
two characteristics effectively removed other viable software programs
from the market.[39]

One ironic aspect of the computing industry at the time was that the
firms "harmed" by Microsoft's monopoly also decided to grow by join-
ing forces. For instance, AOL bought Netscape (competing browser to
Internet Explorer), then AOL created an alliance with Sun (Java was
a competing software platform), yet AOL still wanted to work with
Microsoft's Internet Explorer to expand AOL's availability as an ISP
through Windows. And software company Oracle bought hardware
company Sun Microsystems, which owned the Java Platform. This
means AOL, Java, Oracle, Netscape, and Sun were all interconnected
by the time Judge Jackson ruled in the case, with one of the companies

insisting that partnering together—and with Microsoft—was actually necessary:

> An internal AOL document says that the acquisition of Netscape and the alliance with Sun is "not about Microsoft. We have always considered Microsoft both a tough competitor and an important partner. This deal doesn't change that. Our intention is to continue to use Microsoft's Internet Explorer within the AOL service, because we believe it is important to have AOL bundled with Windows." Colburn, 6/22/99am, at 6:2–17; DX 2522.[40]

In further irony, *Infoworld* gave its 1999 Award for Industry Achievement to Linus Torvalds, who had created a free operating system as a hobby. The Linux operating system was running on between 10 million and 25 million servers at the time Judge Jackson ruled against Microsoft. Contrary to Gates's assertions starting in 1976, there are individuals who would make completely new operating systems without financial reward. And contrary to Judge Jackson's ruling, innovation would continue to happen in the industry—some of that innovation would be willful competition against various established companies. Petreley states of a person developing a new operating system in the 1990s as a hobby, then letting other people commercialize the product that could be downloaded for free: "In a sense, that makes Torvalds the quintessential anti-Gates. Bill Gates is a contract law genius who was given the persona of a technical whiz by marketing."[41]

JACKSON CAME UNDER FIRE FOR PUTTING GATES UNDER FIRE

While United States District Court judge Thomas Penfield Jackson had supervised cases against Microsoft from the approval of the initial consent decree in 1995—when the previous judge's ruling on the first consent decree had been overruled on appeal—until 2000, there were still more changes to come. As reported by the Berkman Center for Internet & Society at Harvard University,

> Pushing the envelope of the code of conduct that bars judges from public discussion of pending cases, Jackson spoke out about

Microsoft both prior to and after rendering his decision, report-edly comparing its executives to inner-city gang members.[42]

Auletta had written in *Final Offer* about his interactions with Judge Jackson:

> He was only half joking when he told me, "If I were able to pro-pose a remedy of my devising, I'd require Mr. Gates to write a book report." The assignment, Jackson said, would be a recent biography of Napoleon, and he went on, "Because I think he has a Napoleonic concept of himself and his company, an arrogance that derives from power and unalloyed success, with no leavening hard experience, no reverses."[43]

Jackson compared Microsoft executives to five drug gang members who had appeared in his court after assassinating three people, yet didn't see anything wrong with the behavior. He then even questioned the competence of Microsoft's chief lawyer:

> Since the evidence appeared so lopsided, Jackson often wondered why Microsoft didn't abort the trial—and stop the damage to its reputation—by seeking a settlement. He blamed Microsoft's chief counsel, William Neukom, saying that he should have arranged a truce before the financial markets were roiled and a judge was forced to play Solomon. One day, Jackson said of Neukom, "I don't think he's very smart, or at least I don't think he has any subtlety. He's the general counsel of this company. He should have said, 'Look, you may think you're doing the right thing, but there are a lot of people who don't, and the time has come for us to be flexible.'"[44]

APPEALS COURT AND MONOPOLY, AND JACKSON

At the Appeals Court, the judges did not overrule the determination that Microsoft was a monopoly but did issue very precise exact state-ments rebuking the comments Judge Jackson had made outside of court against Gates, his firm, and other Microsoft executives. In fact, Jackson got real-time feedback from the court. If the judge hearing the case could not remain impartial, that act alone would open any ruling made by the judge to further, continuing appeals. Appellate Judge Edwards made the comment that the judicial system would be "sham" if judges spoke about participants in trials in the way Judge Jackson had done. Appellate Judge Sentelle noted that the average citizen could only explain the behavior of Jackson as a form of bias, and Appellate Judge Williams took particular offense to the description of Gates as similar to drug gangs, noting: "He chose a particular metaphor. Metaphors are very powerful. And the metaphor he chose was the one best devised, that you could imagine, except possibly the Holocaust, to indicate that Microsoft was beneath the pale, beyond the pale."[45]

The expression that "Justice Is Blind," with imagery of Lady Justice holding a scale to weigh evidence, is exceptionally important in trials—and appeals—when there is a lack of impartiality or fairness (real or perceived) from the judge or panel of judges. And the Microsoft case was highly visible and impacted a firm worth many billions of dollars. At that point, the writing was on the wall. Judge Jackson would not be supervising the Microsoft case through appeals and a settlement, and the Appeals Court would be "providing feedback" before issuing its next order.

Although the order from the Appeals Court was still months away, on March 12, 2001, Judge Jackson recused himself from two cases involving Microsoft in a *Memorandum*; the antitrust case as well as a discrimination case where Microsoft was the defendant. Given the comments from peers on the Appellate panel, he could judge the tone of their pending ruling. In his order, he stated that due to being the randomly assigned judge after the departure of Judge Sporkin and overseeing the case from 2005 to present:

> Over the course of those prior proceedings, I formed unfavorable judgments as to the lawfulness of Microsoft's business practices. Those judgments are fully reflected in my several opinions in those cases. I also formed—and retain—a further impression of Microsoft, also evident, I believe, from my opinions as well as from any public statements attributed to me after the trial. That impression is of a company with an institutional disdain for both

the truth and for rules of law that lesser entities must respect. It is also a company whose "senior management" is not averse to offering specious testimony to support spurious defenses to claims of its wrongdoing.[46]

Under U.S. law, a judge is allowed to form an exceptionally strong opinion against a firm when based upon the evidence in an existing trial. Jackson believed that Microsoft and its unnamed "senior management"— which would include Gates—would not follow the rule of law if that were to benefit the company. And finding that Microsoft leadership was less-than-forthcoming in the antitrust trial would be allowed based upon the evidence. The problem would be if these opinions of Microsoft would prevent Jackson from evaluating cases involving the firm fairly in the future: "Only if the judge's opinions reflect "deep-seated and unequivocal antagonism that would render fair judgment impossible" in such circumstances is recusal required for actual personal bias or prejudice."[47]

Jackson believed his conduct had not risen to that level but the popular perception was to the contrary, noting that comments he made outside the courtroom had been rebuked by the court of appeals.

I do not believe my lingering impressions of Microsoft rise to that level. I must acknowledge, however, that extra-judicial comments attributed to me, when viewed in light of the public disapproval thereof expressed by the court of appeals at oral argument of the *Microsoft* cases appeal, have created an appearance of personal bias or prejudice.[48]

The Appellate Court returned the case back to the U.S. District Court, without Judge Jackson, on June 28, 2001, to seek a new round of litigation. However, Microsoft was still deemed by the Appeals Court to have used monopoly power against almost every conceivable company and vendor in the computing industry at the time, ranging from hardware producers to Internet providers to authors and software companies: "Microsoft, the Appeals Court found, unfairly used its monopoly power to strong-arm computer manufacturers, Internet access providers, Internet content providers, independent software venders, and companies like AOL, Apple, Intel, and Sun Microsystems."[49]

Judge Colleen Kollar-Kotelly was the third judge randomly assigned to the case (after Sporkin, then Jackson). She entered the final judgment[50] against Microsoft on November 12, 2002, agreeing to what—after many years of proceedings and negotiations—was referred to as the TRPFJ ("Third Revised Proposed Final Judgment") in the accompanying order.[51]

As we know now, Microsoft was not required to break up and was primarily using a settlement that had been inherited from the DOJ as composed in the Clinton administration. The judge faced some criticism for not imposing greater sanctions on the company to stop some behaviors by Microsoft, but she quickly dispelled critics by noting that Microsoft could not be punished for actions that had not been proven at trial or at the Appeals Court; that was outside the scope of her charge when the case was returned.

While noting that Microsoft had broken the law, she found that the company had abused its power in the market but had not abused the customers. "Judge Kollar-Kotelly did note that Microsoft 'has a tendency to minimize the effects of its illegal conduct' and had showed a 'paternalistic view' toward consumers."[52]

The judge did make two new innovative components of the settlement, though. The first consent decree applied only to consumer versions of Windows, but the judge ruled the second consent decree would also apply to versions of Windows that ran on servers. The second addition from the judge required Microsoft Windows to allow applications created by other firms to run when the computer is started.

> At least one Microsoft competitor voiced enthusiasm for Judge Kollar-Kotelly's decision. RealNetworks said the judge's requirement that Microsoft allow competing programs to start automatically when a computer is booted up could be a useful edge for the company's audio and video playback software. That obligation goes beyond what was required of the company in the settlement.[53]

Microsoft accepted the settlement and knew that the future looked a lot better as a result of avoiding the break-up proposed by Judge Jackson: "While putting new responsibilities on Microsoft, this settlement also gives us the freedom to keep innovating for our customers," Microsoft's chairman, Bill Gates, said at a news conference at the company's headquarters in Redmond, Wash. "We're pleased to put another step of this case behind us."[54]

Gates spent years defending the actions of his company against the government, when he felt consumers were benefiting from the products Microsoft created. And the efforts took a toll on him. After leading the firm for more than two decades, he was quoted in *Microsoft Rebooted* as saying "by '99 a combination of the lawsuit and some impact of the lawsuit going on . . . meant that I was enjoying my job less than I had in previous years. . . . I still . . . loved the job. It's just that I didn't feel like I was on everything as I like to be."[55] The competitive nature of Gates found the work rewarding but not at the same intensity as in the past.

His family also noticed changes in Bill, with the stress and energy expended in the trial. Father Bill Gates Sr. was similarly quoted in *Microsoft Rebooted*, admitting to feeling "a sense of relief after what he went through" throughout the process of the trial.[56] While Microsoft had largely defined Bill Gates over a period of 25 years, he still had other projects and work to undertake.

LEGACY OF BILL GATES, IMMEDIATELY POST-TRIAL

After the bruising Microsoft trial, threat of the company being split, and his departure as chief executive officer, one might think that Gates would not be treated well by history, or historians, or even business historians. In fact, shortly after the 2002 Microsoft settlement, McCormick and Folsom conducted a survey to assess who business historians would evaluate as the greatest entrepreneurs and businesspeople in U.S. history.

Entrepreneurs were defined as risk-takers and creators, while the businesspeople were defined as managers or financiers. In their survey of 58 historians asking about the greatest entrepreneurs and businesspeople throughout the entirety of American History, Bill Gates placed second on the ranking behind only Henry Ford. More surprisingly, Bill Gates was the only living person listed in the top 14 (and Warren Buffett was not on the list at all as a businessperson). None of the top five entrepreneurs in the ranking system (Ford, Gates, Rockefeller, Carnegie, or Edison) were college graduates.

One of the respondents to their survey had noted the importance of entrepreneurs; while politicians were often given credit and ranked highly, politicians could do nothing without the resources created by the risk-takers over time:

When it comes to our standard of living and quality of life, most Americans ascribe far too much to politicians and far too little to our great entrepreneurs. The latter take the risks and push the envelope, conquering obstacles, and enriching our lives every day of the week. Politicians, even the best of them, can [only] rearrange and redistribute the good things that entrepreneurs create. . . .[57]

THE END OF SANCTIONS UNDER THE SECOND CONSENT DECREE

One might be surprised to learn that Microsoft was under sanctions for a very long time after the Microsoft antitrust trial was finally "settled" in 2002. In fact, some monitoring processes from the DOJ were extended, and Microsoft was not released from sanctions until May 12, 2011: 16 years after Judge Jackson inherited the Microsoft case, 13 years after Bill Gates's deposition, 11 years after Bill Gates vacated the CEO position for Steve Ballmer, and 3 years after Gates had retired from full-time work with Microsoft. The DOJ then stated:

Microsoft no longer dominates the computer industry as it did when the complaint was filed in 1998. Nearly every desktop middleware market, from web browsers to media players to instant messaging software, is more competitive today than it was when the final judgment was entered. In addition, the final judgment helped create competitive conditions that enabled new kinds of products, such as cloud computing services and mobile devices, to develop as potential platform threats to the Windows desktop operating system.

The core allegation in the original lawsuit, upheld by the U.S. Court of Appeals in June 2001, was that Microsoft had unlawfully maintained its monopoly in PC operating systems by excluding competing middleware that posed a nascent threat to the Windows operating system. Specifically, the court of appeals upheld the district court's conclusion that Microsoft engaged in unlawful exclusionary conduct by using contractual provisions to prohibit computer manufacturers from supporting competing middleware products on Microsoft's operating system, prohibiting consumers and computer manufacturers from removing access to Microsoft's middleware products in the operating system, and reaching agreements with software developers and third parties to exclude or impede competing middleware products.[58]

On the occasion of the expiration of the second consent decree (and extensions), Microsoft released the following statement: "Our experience has changed us and shaped how we view our responsibility to the industry. We are pleased to bring this matter to successful resolution, and we are excited to keep delivering great products and services for our partners and customers."[59]

Upon the expiration of the sanctions on May 12, 2011, Microsoft was no longer under any monitoring process from the DOJ but had spent more than two consecutive decades—over half the corporation's lifetime-to-date—under investigation or a consent decree, a rarity in corporate history.

Chapter 7

STEVE JOBS AND BILL GATES

For all of the belief that Microsoft and Apple were long-term competitors, in fact the relationship between Bill Gates and Apple's cofounder Steve Jobs went back decades, from the dawn of the micro-computing age in 1975 through Jobs's death in 2011. Microsoft even developed software for Apple, and the biggest innovations for each firm were inspired by Xexox's PARC (Palo Alto Research Center) site, where each was able to see early versions of graphical user interfaces (GUIs) for computers, the predecessors to the computers we use today rather than screens that only create output in terms of text.

This does not mean that Apple and Microsoft were always friendly, or that the nature of their competition never changed. In fact, the two companies were most closely integrated during the timeframe Jobs was at Apple, rather than the 11-year period between 1985 and 1996 when Jobs had been exiled from his own company. After Gates decided to leave the role of CEO, he frequently interacted with Jobs, showing appreciation for the capability and renaissance Jobs led at Apple as well as verbal jabs when needed to defend his company.

THE iERA OF PRODUCT EVOLUTION

Publicly, Bill Gates had to defend the company he cofounded against major innovations created by Apple under the Steve Jobs–led resurgence. First came the iPod in 2004, allowing consumers to take digital music anywhere with a small device. Despite Gates's contention that the iPod was within Microsoft's capability and that consumers would likely look for alternatives rather than an identical device, the media product created by Microsoft as an alternative—the Zune—was far less successful than the iPod. Gates dismissed the initial iPod with:

> There's nothing that the iPod does that I say, "Oh, wow, I don't think we can do that." "There's often, early in the new market, a few products that help get the category to critical mass. In the long run, people are going to buy what gives them the right price, performance, and capabilities. And does everybody want to have exactly the same thing? Probably not"[1]

The next major Apple release of the first decade of the 2000s was the iPhone. A Microsoft engineer inadvertently—and indirectly—launched that idea. The engineer, who developed the tablet PC, was married to a friend of Steve Jobs. The engineer kept talking about the tablet PC he developed for Microsoft at a birthday party that was attended by both Gates and Jobs. Neither Gates nor Jobs was happy, according to Isaacson, but for different reasons. Gates did not like disclosing intellectual property.

"He's our employee and he's revealing our intellectual property," Gates recounted.[2]

Jobs was unhappy hearing about the Microsoft tablet project and the insistence from Gates's staff that using a stylus as pen was the direction of the future for tablets, so he ordered his staff to create a touch screen. Apple then realized the phone might have more immediate appeal than the tablet. Apple really created the touch-screen interface that was first used for the iPhone, then iPad, because Steve Jobs was upset at listening to a Microsoft engineer at an event attended by Bill Gates.

Gates seemed to appreciate the level of innovation and sophistication of the iPhone in 2007, which had the touch screen that Jobs ordered his staff to create after the party, although Gates may not have known the original source of Jobs's inspiration for the touch screen at the time. Instead of Gates lobbing a missive at Apple's product, Microsoft CEO Steve Ballmer took the lead in disparaging the iPhone before it was released:

> There's no chance that the iPhone is going to get any significant market share. No chance. It's a $500 subsidized item. They may make a lot of money. But if you actually take a look at the 1.3 billion phones that get sold, I'd prefer to have our software in 60% or 70% or 80% of them, than I would to have 2% or 3%, which is what Apple might get.[3]

Microsoft did not do well in creating a market for phones running Windows, eventually buying Nokia in 2013. The next stop for Apple was the iPad in 2010, which Gates did not appreciate at all. Still preferring a netbook plus that stylus he saw as important—instead of a touchscreen—he admitted that the iPhone from 2007 was much scarier to him than the iPad:

> "You know, I'm a big believer in touch and digital reading, but I still think that some mixture of voice, the pen and a real keyboard—in other words a netbook—will be the mainstream on that," he said. "So, it's not like I sit there and feel the same way I did with iPhone where I say, 'Oh my God, Microsoft didn't aim high enough.' It's a nice reader, but there's nothing on the iPad I look at and say, 'Oh, I wish Microsoft had done it.'"[4]

GATES AND JOBS APPRECIATION PROGRAM

In 2007 at the *All ThingsD Conference*, Gates and Jobs sat on a stage for a joint interview, where each was able to easily recognize the achievements of the other and contribution to the industry. Jobs started by saying that the concept of a software company really did not exist before Gates: "Well, you know, Bill built the first software company in the industry and I think he built the first software company before anybody really in our industry knew what a software company was, except for these guys."[5]

Gates similarly expressed opinions on the early Apple computers introduced in the 1970s:

> What Steve's done is quite phenomenal, and if you look back to 1977, that Apple II computer, the idea that it would be a mass-market machine, you know, the bet that was made there by Apple uniquely—there were other people with products, but the idea that this could be an incredible empowering phenomenon, Apple pursued that dream.[6]

Jobs was able to articulate that Microsoft benefited from the partnership with Apple; in fact, Microsoft only focused on programming languages and operating systems before developing software applications for the Mac, as Lotus was the biggest name for software on the PC. Jobs also brought up the partnership that was initiated in 1997, joking that he had been married to Gates for the past decade. Jobs also realized the importance of working with Gates and what the role of Apple had to be at that time to improve the company's future: "But Apple didn't have to beat Microsoft. It had to remember what Apple was. Microsoft was the biggest software developer around, and Apple was weak. So I called Bill up."[7]

Reflecting a comment Gates had made elsewhere about the microcomputing revolution, Jobs saw that he had gone from being the youngest person in the room in 1975 to the oldest in the room in 2007. And if Jobs had lived longer, we might have seen what he had meant by the expression "a phone as a post-PC device."

Gates also showed that he continued to expect innovations to come from outside Microsoft, and that those innovations are beneficial to promoting the continued use of personal computers: "Well, there's always going to be great new things that come out of other companies, and you want to be in a position to benefit from those, to have those inventions drive demand for Windows and personal computers and then some of those upstream things you want to participate in."[8]

LAST TALK AMONG FRIENDS

Of the last time Bill Gates and Steve Jobs talked before Jobs's death, Gates made an astute observation that had been clearly connected to the success cycles of Apple over the years. Apple had made a reputation for designing and putting together hardware and software into packages, with Gates adding, "The integrated approach works when Steve is at the helm. But it doesn't mean it will win many rounds in the future";[9] Gates saw that his model of working with many hardware configurations had worked well for Microsoft, but Jobs was the sole reason the combination of function and design on hardware and software was successful.

On the death of Jobs in October 2011, Gates posted a small note on his personal website, noting the impact of Jobs in the nearly 30 years the two had been acquainted.[10] In fact, Gates and Jobs had known each other for more than 30 years as early innovators in the industry, and Jobs was 56 (Gates was about to reach his 56th birthday); IBM had launched the PC just over 30 years prior. In an interview with Gates shortly after the death of Jobs, *ABC News'* Delawala brought up a statement attributed to Jobs in Isaacson's biography *Steve Jobs*, which had just been released: "Bill is basically unimaginative and has never invented anything, which is why I think he's more comfortable now in philanthropy than technology. He just shamelessly ripped off other people's ideas." Graciously, Gates accepted the criticism and noted that each had made complimentary—and not so complimentary—statements about the other. "Over the course of the 30 years we worked together, you know, he said a lot of very nice things about me and he said a lot of tough things. We got to work together. We spurred each other on, even as competitors. None of that bothers me at all." Gates even accepted the fact that Jobs felt that Apple was good and Microsoft was evil, saying "at various times, he felt beleaguered, he felt like he was the good guy and we were the bad guys, you know, very understandable."[11]

Gates was already likely aware of Jobs's beliefs that Bill was exceptional at business but could have been far more exceptional when talking about the product. "They were never as ambitious product-wise as they should have been. Bill likes to portray himself as a man of the product, but he's really not. He's a businessperson. Winning business was more important than making great products."[12]

Later, it was revealed that Gates had written a letter to Jobs congratulating him on the company he had built and his family, as friends rather than competitors, as Jobs was dying: "After Jobs's death, Gates received a phone call from his wife, Laurene. She said; 'Look, this biography really doesn't paint a picture of the mutual respect you had.' And she said he'd appreciated my letter and kept it by his bed."[13]

Chapter 8

BILL GATES IN WRITINGS

The most meaningful way to differentiate your company from your competition, the best way to put distance between you and the crowd, is to do an outstanding job with information. How you gather, manage, and use information will determine whether you win or lose.[1]

Bill Gates's writings include the following:

The Open Letter to Hobbyists, in 1976, Microsoft's first year
The Road Ahead, in 1995
The Road Ahead: Completely Revised and Up-to-Date, in 1996
Business @ the Speed of Thought, in 1999
The Trustworthy Computing Memo, January 2002

Mr. Gates has multiple writings, including one 1995 book that projected his vision of the future of technology.

Bill Gates was seen as a visionary in some aspects of technology, but he was often a little behind in recognizing patterns. He has co-written two of books; one most notably is *The Road Ahead* in 1995. At the same time, Windows 95 was also being released (August 24, 1995), with the very first version of the Internet Explorer web browser. The bundling of Internet Explorer with the Windows operating system was a fairly novel idea in 1995.

The age of the Internet as most users know from web browsing is relatively new in the history of computing. While there were ISPs before 1993, the Internet was exceptionally limited. A commercial, for-profit company was not even allowed to operate on the Internet due to the operating agreement until April 1993. The earliest for-profit companies we know today with online presences—like Yahoo!—were established shortly thereafter in 1994.

In those early days of the Internet, users with computers may or may not be connected consistently. In December 1995, there were a total of just 16 million users online, which was less than one-half of 1 percent of the world's population. While the tool was quickly becoming more useful, the product was a specialized market with few organizations attempting to make profit online. By the end of 1998, 147 million users were on the Internet, then 3.6 percent of the world's population. By early 2013, there were 2.5 billion users on the Internet; 2,500 million or more than one-third of the world's population. As a result of this rapid growth, many businesses have changed models over time.

The original browser with image capability was called NCSA Mosaic, released in 1993. Before that time, all webpages could include only text in browsers like Lynx. Over time, extensions of the Mosaic product were labelled Netscape with a branch now called Firefox. Another path was that of Microsoft Internet Explorer.

The Microsoft Corporation did not develop its own web browser originally. A firm called Spyglass was a startup initiated by the University of Illinois at Urbana-Champaign; that firm licensed the NCSA Mosaic product and made modifications, and the modified product was licensed by Microsoft as Internet Explorer. Like with previous innovations such as the need to develop an operating system for IBM a decade and a half prior, the company did rely upon the expertise of others in order to create the product that was needed. Microsoft did recognize the importance of the Internet, but Bill Gates admits he was not the one who made the connection.

INTERNET LEADING A REVOLUTION

Robert Kahn and Vinton Cerf, two of the originators of the Internet as we know it today—wrote about a very innovative individual in the 1970s who saw the ability to use technology and computers to connect government agencies and educational institutions, building a highly competitive economic system.

> The name is not Gates, Allen, Ballmer, or anyone else at
>   Microsoft.
> The name is not Jobs or Wozniak or anyone else at Apple.

The name is Al Gore Jr., former senator from the state of Tennessee, former vice president of the United States, and the 2000 nominee for president of the United States. He coined the phrase "information highway" a little before the use by Bill Gates in 1995. And by a little while ago, Microsoft was still located in Albuquerque in the late 1970s.

The Internet innovators wrote of Gore, "As far back as the 1970s Congressman Gore promoted the idea of high speed telecommunications as an engine for both economic growth and the improvement of our educational system. He was the first elected official to grasp the potential of computer communications to have a broader impact than just improving the conduct of science and scholarship. Though easily forgotten now, at the time this was an unproven and controversial concept."[2]

Innovation may take time, and the ways in which the Internet may be used were no exception. Looking at the dates your favorite companies developed their online websites, you might notice that the years start in the mid-1990s. For instance, Yahoo! and Amazon were founded in 1994; Google was founded in 1998. There is an exceptionally good reason these popular sites did not exist before then; an agreement to allow the commercial use of the Internet was not made until March 1993. Without businesses on the Internet, the uses were often government, scientific research, colleges/universities, and open discussion groups but no commerce. Usage stats drastically increased afterward.[3]

THE ROAD AHEAD, FIRST EDITION IN 1995 (THERE WERE TWO)

This one (revolution) will involve unprecedentedly inexpensive communication; all the computers will join together to communicate with us and for us. Interconnected globally, they will form a network, which is being called the information highway. A direct precursor is the present Internet, which is a group of computers joined and exchanging information using current technology.[4]

As a revolution, Gates spoke about many ideas that were difficult to implement with technology in 1995 but much easier today. He noted that while adults might have trouble adapting to using computers and various information tools, children born later would be able to readily use technology to communicate and work without much difficulty.

He stated that the two biggest factors in the workplace would be related to productivity (given ready access to vast quantities of information) and changes in work interactions due to networking. He also saw the potential for an increasingly connected workforce to begin working remotely, noting that there would be many potential social, economic, and environmental aspects resulting from these new ways of

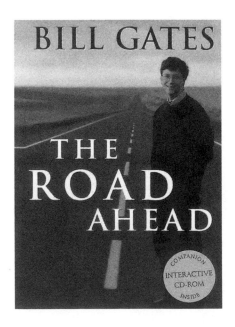

While Gates had already been shaping the computing industry for two decades, The Road Ahead *was his first foray into writing best-selling books.* (AP Photo/HO)

communicating and working. For instance, individuals could live further from the traditional place of employment, traffic could be lessened by remote workers, and air pollution would be decreased.

Gates did not see technology as a panacea, though. He did worry that improvements in technology and communication could cause more affluent people to leave cities, which could harm the tax base and other citizens. Another worry—when most people still were not on the Internet—was the concessions that would need to be made for security, both wired and wireless: "Wireless service poses obvious concerns about privacy and security, because radio signals can easily be intercepted. Even wired networks can be tapped. The highway software will have to encrypt transmission to avoid eavesdropping."

And he even talks about personal frustrations and beliefs along the way, ranging down to a traffic light that stays on red for an unacceptable amount of time near his office. There are little human touches with his writing that are always present; some reviewers see these examples as contrived to add personality into his work.

He did envision that the information highway would best be used in education, so he donated his revenue from the book to teachers who were using computers in the classroom, citing the opportunity he had in computing because the Mothers' Club at Lakeside School had provided a computer where he refined his skills. He similarly donated the funds from his book four years later, *Business @ the Speed of Thought.*

In the afterword, Bill Gates also shared a fear, which is present in many of the other comments he has made over the years. He noted, "My focus is to keep Microsoft in the forefront through constant renewal. It's a little scary that as computer technology has moved ahead there's never been a leader from one era who was also a leader in the next." The concern that Microsoft could always be surpassed and made irrelevant is a consistent theme for Gates.[5]

In addition, Gates shares a vision of what his home—then under construction—would look like and how he would incorporate technology now that he expected to be prevalent in all homes of the future, although he does make a concession that his wealth permits activities not yet available to others.

CALLS FOR DETOURS

Gates immediately faced criticism for the book among some reviewers, who dismissed the book as simultaneously unable to separate the technology and business components of the book. In the *American Spectator*, Joe Queenan included in a withering review of the line "though billed as Gates's personal vision of the electronic future, The Road Ahead is basically 286 pages of shilling for Microsoft and the Internet" and later the missive:

> Though he would dearly like to think of himself as a visionary, Bill Gates's talent has always been marketing, not technology. The genius of Microsoft has never been to arrive at the cutting edge before its competitors, but to convince its customers that it has: Witness the triumph of Windows over Apple's vastly superior operating system. Gates would like to think of himself as Johann Gutenberg or Thomas Edison. But he's really just a hi-tech Ray Kroc. He has one basic talent: He knows how to move the merchandise.[6]

In fact, the reviewer forgot who had worked extensively with Apple in the development of the operating system, that the book was not about the Internet itself but an extension of what the current Internet was, and that Bill Gates had indeed done something that Apple had not done since the departure of Steve Jobs in 1985, which was to sell massive quantities of products at the price points consumers desired. Jobs was about to return to make Apple competitive, with the $150 million investment from Microsoft. Queenan did—inadvertently—get something exceptionally right in the review. Although the book was not about the Internet per se, people who were just connecting to the Internet liked the current Internet sufficiently well to avoid going toward Gates's highway, which became apparent almost immediately.

THE ROAD AHEAD, SECOND EDITION IN 1996 (OR TAKE TWO)

So why was there a second edition to *The Road Ahead*? The road had changed, and the road changed rapidly. In fact, the second edition has a subtitle not present on the first edition, and that was *Completely Revised and Up-to-Date*. The first edition was published in 1995, and the revised version was published the next year. Gates initially thought the information highway would be an extension of the current Internet. Not only was the Internet a complete game-changer in how individuals used computers and technology, adoption was much more rapid than Bill Gates had expected. The current Internet was making those who connected happy, so the leader of Microsoft had to re-envision the vision.

Recall in 1995, Gates had told Don Tennant in an interview "an Internet browser is a trivial piece of software"; Microsoft was at tremendous risk in the antitrust trial due to this very software—Microsoft Internet Explorer—in 1998, as the company leadership was unwilling to cede control of how users were able to make Internet connections. The second edition varies from the first in terms of content and even chapter titles, and the description of the Gates home even has different visuals included as examples, although still had problems predicting how the Internet would evolve; even the most straightforward paragraph from the first edition was modified for the second edition. The inability to precisely define how the Internet would develop is actually a benefit in hindsight; claims that Gates—or Microsoft—manipulated the way users chose to use the Internet can be readily refuted. Some applications that Gates projected have disappeared, replaced by compelling alternatives.

Gates—years later—noted that Microsoft had not been perfect and had missed many large changes over the years but did not enumerate what he thought were his firm's failings: "When we miss a big change, when we don't get great people on it, that is the most dangerous thing for us," Gates said. "It has happened many times. It's OK, but the less the better."[7]

BUSINESS @ THE SPEED OF THOUGHT, 1999

In his next best-selling book, Gates describes the "digital nervous system" he had mentioned in his November 1997 report to shareholders at the Microsoft annual meeting, as well as previously at the 1997 CEO Summit. Ostensibly by then, his business guidance would be less important to competitors, or would at minimum placate competitors during the Microsoft antitrust trial.

The digital nervous system is based upon how information flows through companies, and Gates believed there should be "maximum and constant learning." He stressed that in an increasingly competitive business environment, "how you gather, manage, and use information will determine whether you win or lose."

In a diagram, he articulates how precisely he believes his digital nervous system works, with "the digital processes that closely link every aspect of a company's thoughts and actions. Basic operations such as finance and production, plus feedback from customers, are electronically accessible to a company's knowledge workers, who use digital tools to quickly adapt and respond. The immediate availability of accurate information changes strategic thinking from a separate, stand-along activity to an ongoing process integrated with regular business activities." He explicitly refers to businesses that hire consultants and then must pull together information just for those consultants; given this information is gathered through a special process, the information has not been available consistently for real-time feedback and use by internal decision-makers.

He also makes some errant comments along the way, commending the IT capability of a soon-to-fail Saturn that followed the model he described, and spoke about the need to transmit bad news rapidly, while facing a federal antitrust suit. Speaking about his belief that the company could always fail, he may have been attempting to catch the attention of judges or industry observers. "One day somebody will catch us napping. One day an eager upstart will put Microsoft out of business. I just hope it's fifty years from now, not two or five."[8]

Gates was insistent in many venues that the software written by Microsoft—the entirety of the company's intellectual property—would have no value in five years' time and would require constant innovation and renewal: "There's not a single line of code here today that will have value in, say, four or five years' time. Today's operating systems will be obsolete in five years."[9]

He also speaks about failures at Microsoft, including Multiplan's inability to compete against Lotus 1–2–3, another database called Omega, an early personal digital assistant, and even OS/2 as the "long-term operating system strategy" where Microsoft had invested hundreds of millions of dollars; in *The Road Ahead* only the $2 billion spent by IBM, which was paying Microsoft, was mentioned.[10]

Gates also notes that something had occurred in 1995 that required the massive revision to *The Road Ahead* in 1996, without referring the reader back to that book:

> By late fall, the Internet phenomenon had eclipsed Windows 95 as the industry's story of the year.
>
> On December 7, 1995, we held our first Internet Strategy Day, where for the first time we publicly previewed the array of technologies we were developing to integrate Internet support into our core products.[11]

BUSINESS @ THE SPEED OF THOUGHT, CRITICISM, 1999

Gates's work immediately received both praise and criticism. Some wondered how Gates could get through the entire book without mentioning the active Department of Justice investigation at all, even mentioning critics and companies involved in the antitrust litigation as examples of firms applying the principles he was espousing, and wondered how Gates was willing to write a book about the use of electronic communication—or even think of using e-mail—after the deposition and e-mails were read in trial: "You might think a man who has had his company e-mail captured by the government, read aloud in a courtroom and printed around the world would be put off electronic messaging for life. But Gates the author adores the medium."

Going further, Gates talks about the way his competitors—like those involved in the antitrust trial—use technology in the way he promotes. During an antitrust trial, speaking about how one's competitors operate might be seen as a disadvantage. As a matter of practice, Gates's praising the companies who were testifying against him may have been a strategic choice: "Now Bill the tousle-haired billionaire is back, bursting with business advice and all the exuberance of a boy genius. Sun, Apple, IBM and Intel are merely examples of companies that use digital nervous systems. You'd never guess they also play a major part in the feds' case."[12]

Seven years later in 2006, Gates wrote a "How I Work" narrative, with the insistence on using e-mail as the most common method of communication at Microsoft, where even faxes and voicemail messages were directly tied to e-mail:

> At Microsoft, e-mail is the medium of choice, more than phone calls, documents, blogs, bulletin boards, or even meetings (voicemails and faxes are actually integrated into our e-mail in-boxes).
>
> I get about 100 e-mails a day. We apply filtering to keep it to that level; e-mail comes straight to me from anyone I've ever corresponded with, anyone from Microsoft, Intel, HP, and all the other partner companies, and anyone I know.[13]

In this 2006 example, Gates does describe precisely a future he had written about a decade earlier in *The Road Ahead* as e-mail prescreening. Of course, Gates had already been using e-mail for at least 18 years at the time, based upon the 1988 *Success Magazine* interview.

THE TRUSTWORTHY COMPUTING MEMO

In January 2002, Chief Software Architect (no longer CEO) Gates sent the Trustworthy Computing Memo to all full-time workers at Microsoft. In the memo, he draws connections to systems we accept as reliable and secure in the United States, such as basic utilities. If Microsoft cannot achieve this goal, then people would be unwilling or unable to use Microsoft products. In order to achieve the level of trust Gates deemed necessary, the products should always be available with no system outages and automatic recovery, secure to protect user data, and permit users to control their own level of privacy and how their data may—or may not—be used. Gates saw implementing this framework as more important than adding new features to existing software, and that the need was exacerbated by "weekly" announcements of new security vulnerabilities on various computing platforms—not just Windows—and how the events of 2001 had reminded everyone of the immediate need to always protect the critical infrastructure.[14]

Chapter 9

FAMILY AND HOME OF BILL

Mr. Gates marries and has children in the 1990s.

Michael Eisner wrote in *Working Together, Why Great Partnerships Succeed* that Bill Gates always has at least one exceptionally capable partner. Starting at 1987, the current of these exceptional everyday partners for Bill Gates is Melinda Gates (née French), and this partnership has continued through their 1994 wedding, building of a home designed by Bill and refined by Melinda on Lake Washington, three children, and the current initiative of the Bill and Melinda Gates Foundation.[1] Melinda—due to her influence as co-chair of the Bill and Melinda Gates Foundation—was ranked by *Forbes* in 2013 as the third most powerful woman in the world. While there are references in this chapter to the Bill and Melinda Gates Foundation, the Foundation itself is discussed in Chapter 12 of this book; Gates has declared that his full-time job for the rest of his life resides with the Foundation.

MEETING MELINDA

He met his wife in 1987 at a Microsoft press event in Manhattan. She was working for the company and later became one of the executives in charge of interactive content: "When we very first met, I had worked at the company for only a few weeks. My background was computer science and business school, so eventually I worked my way up where I was running product groups—development, testing, marketing, user education."[2]

Many records detail that Bill and Melinda were married in Lanai, Hawai'i, on January 1, 1994. However, Gates took exceptional steps to protect his privacy, and the privacy of his guests, which included many luminaries.

> Bill and Melinda were married on the golf course belonging to the Manele Bay Hotel in Lanai, Hawaii. To ensure privacy, Gates had taken all 250 rooms at the hotel—including his own $1,300-a-night suite. He also booked all helicopter services on Maui to prevent photographers from renting them. Willie Nelson provided the entertainment. Among the attendees were Warren Buffett, Paul Allen, and Gates's best man, Steve Ballmer.[3]

Bill's mother Mary, who had consistently asked her son to become involved in charitable initiatives, was dying of cancer at the time of

A week after their Hawai'i wedding, Bill Gates and Melinda French Gates host a reception in Seattle. (AP Photo/Dave Weaver)

the wedding. She wrote a toast to the new couple, acknowledging the way Melinda and Mary had interacted, as well as the way Mary had interacted with Bill Sr. over the years. She referred to a part of the wedding vow:

"In sickness and in health"

As you know in the last few months, we have had a chance to reflect quite directly on promises to stand by one another in sickness and in health. This challenge has brought a new depth to our relationship.

Of course, the waters have not always been smooth, but I can't imagine not being married to Bill! I hope you will have this same feeling 42 years from now about your Bill Gates."[4]

Mary Gates passed away shortly thereafter on June 11, 1994.

After the wedding, Melinda continued to work at Microsoft and was one of the marketing managers when Microsoft Bob was released in January 1995. Microsoft Bob was the first time Bill Gates was on stage to launch a product, as Steve Jobs became known for doing later: "Microsoft Bob, an early "user interface," a smiley face with glasses, was introduced in January 1995. One of its marketing managers was Melinda French Gates, Bill's wife. Bob was the first consumer product Gates launched personally."

Microsoft Bob was not a successful product for the firm and was gone within two years. Gates had presided over the product launch but he later joked: "Unfortunately, the software demanded more performance than typical computer hardware could deliver at the time and there wasn't an adequately large market," he wrote. "Bob died."[5]

Working through ideas for their Foundation, he wrote that the couple forms a highly functioning team, where one tempers the enthusiasm of the other by making sure all relevant issues are being considered: "She and I enjoy sharing ideas and talking about what we are learning. When one of us is being very optimistic, the other takes on the role of making sure we're thinking through all the tough issues."[6]

In 2013, Melinda was ranked by *Forbes* magazine as the third most powerful woman in the world and highest-ranking nonpolitician. With the Foundation funded by the couple's amassed fortune, the profile notes the Gates Foundation has to take risks and accept that some of the projects that are funded will be failures: "We not only accept that, we expect it because we think an essential role of philanthropy is to make bets on promising solutions that governments and businesses can't afford to make."[7]

CHILDREN OF BILL AND MELINDA

The Gates family has three children, Jennifer Katharine was born in April 1996, Rory John was born in May 1999, and Phoebe Adele was born in September 2002. Much like Bill's own childhood, the only male child is the middle sibling. While the children do frequently accompany the family on excursions related to the parents' involvement with the Bill and Melinda Gates Foundation, father and mother rarely refer to the children by name in the press, usually referring to their children by age in each conversation. And there's an effort by the family to ensure that the children have opportunities, but they will have to work and won't inherit the family fortune.

Bill Gates was the subject of a parody website www.billg.com, which was online for a number of years with weekly updates. Gates was consistently described as socially inept and geeky, and his actual attorneys even wrote to the anonymous editor of the website—through the ISP (Internet Service Provider) hosting the website—threatening invasion of privacy and false statements. Gates did not like the parody, but his spokesperson stated that the intervention of the lawyers was not about the boss being the subject of the parody. "Bill recognizes he's a public figure. He's fair game. The issue was about his wife and his family."[8]

In talking about the children, Bill and Melinda reveal much about social interactions and belief systems. In 1998, Barbara Walters interviewed Gates about his first child, who was then less than two. Gates not only talked about the singing lessons he took with Melinda but also broke into song about the lullabies he sang to his eldest daughter: "I said, 'What do you sing the baby?' Walters said, referring to his 21-month-old daughter, Jennifer Katharine, and Gates broke into a rendition of 'Twinkle Twinkle Little Star.'"[9]

In a 2010 interview, Melinda spoke about efforts ranging from her childhood to the Bill and Melinda Gates Foundation to her family and children. In her religious high school, the school's motto is "Serviam," that is, "I will serve," which has guided her efforts with the Foundation. She continues to be Catholic despite disagreeing with the Church on the issue of reproductive health and birth control.

Promoting women's issues through the Foundation, like the Global Strategy for Women's and Children's Health, was seen as important because of past neglect of women's issues. As she stated, "80 percent of small-subsistence farmers in sub-Saharan Africa are women, and yet all the programs in the past were predominantly focused on men." When questioned why the Foundation doesn't do more in the United States, she noted the three major programs and that approximately one-fifth of all funds were for U.S. programs.

When talking about her family, she provides a lot more personalization. Of being a warmer person than Bill, she relayed that her husband was improving, recently uttering the line: "I'm starting to realize that talking to people about tuberculosis at a cocktail party doesn't go so well." And just like Bill's parents when he was younger, Bill and Melinda speak about topics at the table that would rarely—if ever—be mentioned within most families: "We say at our dinner table, 'Diarrhea is a discussion we can have,'" and the kids will go, 'Ugh!' Diarrhea kills a million and a half kids a year. Sometimes we overdo it, I think, at the dinner table."

The children in the Gates family are not permitted to own Apple products, and Phoebe Adele was noted as teasing him when he fell from the top ranking in the list of the world's billionaires.[10]

Bill maintains that he is not religious but had been given the choice of religions for the children if the family would attend church. When pondering his first child in communication with an author, he wrote: "Religion has come around to the view that even things that can be explained scientifically can have an underlying purpose that goes beyond the science. Even though I am not religious, the amazement and wonder I have about the human mind is closer to religious awe than dispassionate analysis."[11]

Melinda's stories about the children parallel what Bill relates about the children at the same time. In 2010, Travie McCoy and Bruno Mars released the popular music hit *Billionaire*, which is sung often in the Gates household:

> "The Billionaire song is what my kids tease me with," he says. "They sing it to me. It's funny."
>
> They have apparently also introduced him to the "joys" of Lady Gaga, "but the 12-year-old is always worried about the nine-year-old listening to songs with bad words. So he's like, 'No! Skip that one!' So I only know some Lady Gaga songs."[12]

Gates also reiterated that his kids would not become rich via an inheritance, with their educational and health needs covered but each of his children "will have to pick a job they like and go to work. They are normal kids now. They do chores, they get pocket money."

Despite enormous wealth, the default vehicle of the Gates family is a minivan driven by Bill, as the events of the Gates children occupy a lot of his schedule since his retirement from Microsoft full time: "We have a minivan and that's what we use when it's the five of us. My eldest daughter rides horses, so we go to a lot of three-day shows. The kids are a big part of my schedule."[13]

Gates has the resources to make his schedule—and his children's schedules—much less difficult to manage. One of the events where his eldest daughter rides horses is in Wellington, Florida. In 2013, he purchased an existing estate in Florida—one his family had once rented during a competition—to accommodate his daughter's hobby at a cost of $8.7 million, drawing some criticism in the media at the time.[14]

Being a child of Bill Gates does have other benefits. As Bill and Melinda—along with U2's Bono—had been selected to represent *Time's* Person of the Year in 2005, he was asked if Bono had invited the Gates family backstage after a 2011 concert in Seattle. His response to the interviewer's question? "Umm, no—actually, he (Bono) stayed at our house."[15]

His children do attend private schools—as Gates himself had done. However, this has led to criticism in the media, as Gates has described smaller class sizes as a waste of public funding and encouraged larger classes for the most effective teachers in public education.[16]

Despite his technological prowess, Bill mentions still liking to open books despite believing that digital reading will one day be the only option. However, he bristled a bit when asked about the legacy that he was creating:

> Legacy is a stupid thing! I don't want a legacy. If people look and see that childhood deaths dropped from nine million a year to four million because of our investment, then wow! I liken what I'm doing now to my old job. I worked with a lot of smart people; some things went well, some didn't go so well. But when you see how what we did ended up empowering people, it's a very cool thing.[17]

Q&A FOR BILL GATES

In 2012, Gates was asked on his personal website about how the family teaches the children about the initiatives most important to the parents in their new full-time positions with the Bill and Melinda Gates Foundation, and he started by describing how his children react to travelling with the family to areas like Africa and witnessing those environments, asking questions, and making connections. Gates was certain that his children would rapidly learn about the concepts and science behind the work done by their parents:

> They're different ages, but over time they'll learn about the bigger issues, and the science involved. They're interested in seeing things they're studying in school. My daughter is taking a course on African history, so she asks a lot about that. My son is very interested in politics, democracy and the unrest in some countries. He's curious about why some countries have done better than others, like why Turkey is richer than Egypt.[18]

THE WASHINGTON ESTATE OF THE GATES FAMILY

Bill Gates and his family live in a waterfront home in Medina, Washington, just outside Seattle, Washington. The estate sits on Lake Washington, and the combination of buildings has 7 bedrooms and 18.75 bathrooms. According to the most recent property tax records, the estate is assessed for 2014 at $120,558,000, with the property assessed at $21,740,000 and the house/other structures at $98,818,000.[19]

The Gates Estate had to be planned very carefully to fit in the 5-acre site; some of the structures are almost entirely underground to fit into the landscape. Architecture firm Bohlin Cywinski Jackson (BCJ) still includes the work done on the Bill Gates house on its website as an example of its work, labelled solely as "Pacific Rim Estate." BCJ partnered with Cutler Anderson Architects in the design of the project. Awards for the estate include the 1997 National Honor Award from the American Institute of Architects and 1997 Honor Award for Design Excellence from AIA Pennsylvania.

> Past the garage, a massive, curved wood retaining wall and canopy define the stone entry court that leads to reception spaces in the main house. At the lowest level, an indoor swimming pool overlooks a wetland and the lake. A stone and wood anteroom, with shower and sauna, precedes the light-filled pool space. Covered with grass, the pool's roof is supported by timber framing; canted columns are positioned at its northeast corner to support the heaviest load of soil and logs.[20]

The main house was described in other sources, such as the book *Barbarians Led by Bill Gates,* as having the size of some rooms constrained because of the space needed to hide all of the technology Gates used in the home. In his discussions of the house, Gates does not discuss that allegation.

The guest house, 1,700 square feet itself, won the award from the AIA for being "modest" and "not extravagant." However, the guest house was exceptionally high-tech for the 1990s, and was where many sources reported at the time that he wrote his book *The Road Ahead.* The guest house was also built first to allow for some experimentation in terms of technology:

> The guest house does offer sensors that recognize guests and adjust lighting, heating and music to individual preferences; wiring that allows all of the home's various systems to be controlled via laptop; and a comprehensive video and audio library. High-tech panels that will allow visitors to change the room's wall design or "artwork" at will haven't arrived yet.[21]

THE HOUSE IN HIS OWN WORDS

For a person who values privacy when possible, one of the contradictions of Bill Gates is that he provides the most detailed description of his family's Lake Washington home's technology and design in his book *The Road Ahead,* including an example computer rendering of how the structure fits into a hillside. In Chapter 10 "Plugged in at Home," he describes the possibilities of advanced connectedness from the information highway allowing individuals to stay home more often but remain as social as normal. Like the other version of *The Road Ahead*—there are differences in Chapter 10 before the first and revised edition.

He describes basics of the construction and technology, and also relays that the design of the house had started back in the 1980s, with plans that adapted once he became married, began to think of family, and his wife required a workspace. The use of reclaimed lumber in his home appears to be a source of pride, coming from an old lumber mill that was being demolished. He describes intentionally building the home into a hill and being able to look "west over Lake Washington to Seattle to take advantage of the sunset and Olympic Mountain views."

In describing his house—then still under construction—he clearly understood that he was implementing many technological features that would not be available in other houses for many years, and stated that would be much like a world where there's only one telephone. Vast numbers of technologically advanced homes would have many more capabilities once the Internet was better used and more robust.

He notes, "The cutting-edge technology in the house I'm building won't just be for previewing entertainment applications. It will also help meet the usual domestic needs: for heat, light, comfort, convenience, pleasure, and security." He also admits that technology may fail at times and there are reliable alternatives, so the exceptionally high-tech home would still have physical switches to turn lights on/off as needed. He expresses pragmatism in examples other than the light switches, noting that there were items changed after experimentation in the guest house yet still not knowing precisely how the final product would turn out.[22]

In the exceptionally expensive high-tech home, he describes small spaces as well as large spaces; one of these is designed to accommodate up to 100 people at a time. When he wrote about hosting events, the only references were to Microsoft-related activities; his company was present in his mind even when designing and describing his new home.

Gates appears to earnestly believe that the innovations he implements in his house might become commonplace in the future. He talks about an example of William Randolph Hearst in 1925 in the design of a much more ostentatious home. Hearst also saw a limitation in technology at the time, which was related to changing channels on the radio with a manual tuner knob by hand. His response was to simply have many radios in the basement and each was set to a different station—by pressing a button in his room, he could "change the channel" (actually, changing the radio he could hear). Technology did catch up in the intervening years, and radios are now easily adjustable by pressing buttons instead of manually tuners.

Each visitor receives a pin upon entering the home, which connects the user to technology. This includes turning lights on as one walks through the home, having a movie one is watching follow the user seamlessly on televisions from one room to the next, and only ringing the phone nearest to the user—apparently, Gates did not envision the rapid expansion in the prevalence of cellphones that were already available in 1995. The pin also remembers user preferences and controls which features of the home can be accessed.

Access to the various forms of media was a very profound idea in 1995. The thousands of images is very easy to understand, as Bill Gates already owns the company Corbis and has knowledge of Internet browsers that deliver images to users, which did not exist before NCSA's Mosaic. However, the prompt access to recordings, movies, and television programs pre-dated much of the technology that we associate with the ability to select media easily today.

When we think of the ability to select videos, movies, and television programs on demand, the options we readily think of came a few years later. For instance with video and movies, Netflix was founded in 1997 and didn't start delivering video until 1999; Hulu was founded in 2007. In Music, Napster was founded in 1999 and faced legal issues related to file sharing, and Apple's iTunes came along in 2001.

Gates's vision of being able to search for music and video in his home by attributes like colors, actors, or location is like other services we take for granted today. In fact, this description is much like Google searches and indexes; however, Google's founders started working on their first search engine at Stanford in 1996. Apple's Siri application on the iPhone came about in 2011. In various ways, Gates did understand the processes many of us would use to search through information and media in the years to come.

US News and World Report followed in 1997 with an article about the completed home itself. The gatehouse for security functions alone, at 3,000 square feet, exceeded the average home size in the United States, and in the 1990s already had an X-ray machine installed. The article also noted the building does sit in an earthquake zone, so there are architectural features that greatly exceed the standards required for building in that location. Although the Gates's house was described as 11,500 square feet of personal space, their "inner sanctum is surprisingly modest, with four bedrooms and quarters for a nanny." Of the nontraditional components of the house, there was "a trampoline room with a 20-foot ceiling."[23]

TECHNOLOGY FAILURES

In his 1998 interview with Barbara Walters, Gates revealed that there was indeed a downside to the extensive technology in the home, for which he had planned physical switches that could override any technology glitch:

> The first night in his new house, Gates told Walters, he watched a big-screen TV that pops up out of a console in his bedroom. But things went awry when he tried to go to sleep.
> "He couldn't get it to go down, he couldn't get it to turn off, so he just put a big blanket over the thing," she said. Gates has joked that everything from light switches to music speakers goes on and off unexpectedly in the house, which is run by a high-end PC network built on Microsoft's Windows NT system.[24]

Chapter 10

ROLE IN CORPORATE GOVERNANCE, ACTIVISM, AND OUTSIDE INTERESTS OF BILL GATES

In his post-Microsoft role, Mr. Gates has provided his expertise to inspire others, lobbied on behalf of Microsoft, became active in social media, served on the board of directors for Berkshire Hathaway, and moved most of his wealth outside of Microsoft into his private company called Cascade Investment.

INSPIRING OTHER BILLIONAIRES

While Bill Gates is the richest and most famous Harvard dropout, there's a close second in helping to revolutionize how information is used and shared in the modern economy. Mark Zuckerberg, the CEO of Facebook, and Eduardo Saverin, a Facebook cofounder, had an encounter with Bill Gates early in that company's history at Harvard University. In February 2004, Bill Gates gave a talk in the Lowell Lecture Hall that was attended by the two in an era when Facebook had yet to register users off the campus of Harvard University. The site was popular but far from global.

Bill Gates's talk and mannerisms are addressed briefly in the book *Accidental Billionaires* as well as *The Crimson*, Harvard's student newspaper.

The book also mentions how Bill Gates interjected a few jokes along the way, such as dropping out of school because he "had a terrible habit of not going to classes." In addition to cracking jokes, Gates also included:

> some pearls of wisdom—that AI (Artificial Intelligence) was the future, that the next Bill Gates was out there, possibly in that very room. But Eduardo specifically saw Mark perk up when Gates answered a question from one of the audience members about his decision to leave school and start his own company. After hemming and hawing a bit, Gates told the audience that the great thing about Harvard was that you could always come back and finish.[1]

For Zuckerberg as the leader of the fledgling firm, Gates's acknowledgment that the next billionaire technology innovator might be in that audience was influential. And the recognition that the risk could pay off or lead to a return to Harvard later to complete a degree was empowering. For his colleague Saverin, the same interaction was troubling. "Eduardo understood that entrepreneurship meant taking risks—but only to a certain degree. You didn't risk your entire future on something until you figured out how it was going to make you rich."

The article in *The Crimson* provides more details as to projects underway at Microsoft. While Gates had ceded day-to-day control of Microsoft to Steve Ballmer, his involvement with the firm was still apparent based upon his talk. He lamented "the world as a whole has a shortage of elite, computer science people," but responded to one student question that completing the degree at Harvard first would be beneficial, rather than following his own path to founding Microsoft (the path and comments that inspired Facebook's Zuckerberg in the same talk).

Gates showed the audience a Microsoft device that was similar to an iPod, as well as what was called a "smart watch" that had various capabilities. He also reverted to a mantra that he had expressed fairly consistently over the past 30 years related to intellectual property. In this instance, he actually described some of Microsoft's own products allowing the intellectual property of others to be violated, noting that the absence of the use of various digital technology available to prevent illegal file-sharing had "made it too easy for people not to license."[2]

Microsoft did learn to profit from Facebook's model. In fact, Microsoft invested directly in Facebook in 2007, before shares could be bought and sold on a stock exchange. "After a brief and highly public bidding war with Google, Microsoft bought a 1.6 percent stake in the company for 240 million dollars, roughly valuating Facebook at over 15 billion, or more than one hundred times its 150 million dollars in annual revenues."[3] How well did that investment work for Microsoft? Facebook was valued at over $130 billion on January 1, 2014, which suggests that $240 million investment became more than $2 billion in a little more than six years.

WOMEN'S EMPOWERMENT

The mantra of the Bill and Melinda Gates Foundation is that every life has equal value. Gates also believes that everyone in society is a valuable contributor—although flatly stating the vast majority of the population should not be allowed to program computers—and was quoted in the book *Half the Sky* about one of his speeches where the men and women in the audience were segregated:

> Bill Gates recalls once being invited to speak in Saudi Arabia and finding himself facing a segregated audience. Four fifths of the listeners were men, on the left. The remaining one fifth were women, all covered in black cloaks and veils, on the right. A partition separated the two groups. Toward the end, during the question-and-answer session, a member of the audience noted that Saudi Arabia aimed to be one of the top ten countries in the world in technology by 2010 and asked if that was realistic. "Well, if you're not fully utilizing half the talent in the country," said Gates, "you're not going to get too close to the top ten." The small group on the right erupted in wild cheering, while the larger audience on the left applauded tepidly.[4]

ELECTION TO BOARD OF
BERKSHIRE HATHAWAY

In December 2004, Bill Gates was elected to the board of directors of Berkshire Hathaway, the conglomerate run by his bridge partner Warren Buffett. Bill Gates replaced Susan Buffett, Warren's wife who had passed away in July 2004. As reported by *USA Today*,[5] the Berkshire director job does not pay well and Gates does not receive officers and directors insurance for his service—directors of a firm can be held accountable for their actions or omitted duties on a board. Shortly thereafter, Gates resigned from the board of directors of ICOS, which was a biotechnology company later acquired by Eli Lilly. Berkshire Hathaway, as an investment company, owns dozens of companies across a wide array of businesses, such as the BNSF Railroad, Brooks Shoes, GEICO, International Dairy Queen, NetJets, and See's Candies.

LINKEDIN PRESENCE OF BILL GATES

In mid-2013, Bill Gates created a LinkedIn account, where he posts approximately one article a month as an influencer. He speaks about what he has learned and how he envisions making the world a better place through the initiatives where he has passion. After attending the Annual Microsoft Conference for faculty teaching computer science, he posted about how experts in various academic disciplines—such as computer science—could contribute, for instance by developing models on the spread of disease.[6] In another post, he spoke of the three most important things he had learned from Warren Buffett, with the two major takeaways being that Buffett is a highly sophisticated investor— much more so than Gates has originally believed—and that the same approach used for investing makes Buffett an excellent advisor for the Bill and Melinda Gates Foundation's philanthropic efforts.[7]

DWINDLING OWNERSHIP INTEREST IN MICROSOFT

Despite Gates no longer serving as CEO of Microsoft after 2000, he did use the chairman's role between 2000 and 2014 to continually promote the interests of Microsoft. Examples are testimony before Congress at a U.S. competitiveness hearing discussing the need for reform to the H1-B Visa program for talented computer programmers. As Gates stated to Congress, "These top people are going to be hired. It's just a question of what country they're hired in. And if these top engineers are forced to work in India, we will hire students from India to work around them." In other words, Gates was saying that he needed to have employees near the best programmers in the world; if those programmers could not come to the United States, Microsoft would have to allocate more employees abroad to learn from those experts.[8]

Although Gates has expanded involvement in organizations other than Microsoft, he had simultaneously come under criticism for maintaining his role as chairman of Microsoft's board of directors as a result of a few distinct facts: the firm has launched products not seen as overly successful, the departure of Steve Ballmer from the CEO role—which occurred in February 2014—and Gates's own divestment of shares in Microsoft. In fact, disclosures required by the federal government (SEC Form 4s) show that Gates has sold more than 30 percent of his personal shares in Microsoft in a period of less than two years. SEC Form 4s show that Gates's stockholdings in Microsoft have decreased from 515,980,456 shares owned on January 24, 2012[9] to 357,990,173 shares owned on January 1, 2014[10] as part of his scheduled divestment process, with smaller numbers of shares awarded as stock option grants each year. Gates uses the proceeds and his Microsoft dividends to make investments in other firms and contribute to his foundation. If the current rate of divesting shares continues, Gates will own zero shares of Microsoft by 2018.

With Gates's shrinking ownership in Microsoft and ownership of less than 5 percent of the firm, his continued service as chairman of the board of directors at Microsoft and involvement in replacing Steve Ballmer as CEO created a quandary. Upon the announcement of the appointment of Satya Nadella to the role of CEO of Microsoft in February 2014, the firm had elevated a 22-year veteran of the company to the primary leadership role on a day-to-day basis. Concurrent with that announcement, Gates stepped down from the powerful role of chairman of the board of directors and became the technology advisor, a new position that will help guide the new CEO on technology matters but may detract somewhat from what Gates has described as his full-time work from 2008 through the rest of his life: the Bill and Melinda Gates Foundation. Of the new CEO, Gates accentuated characteristics of Nadella that had often been said of himself: "Satya is a proven leader with hard-core engineering skills, business vision and the ability to bring people together. His vision for how technology will be used and experienced around the world is exactly what Microsoft needs as the company enters its next chapter of expanded product innovation and growth."[11]

EXTERNAL SHAREHOLDINGS

Bill Gates now maintains most of his wealth outside of the firm Microsoft. Unlike Microsoft, which is publicly traded and requires extensive reporting, a firm owned by a single individual does not require those forms of disclosures. There are multiple advantages to Mr. Gates for holding his wealth inside a personal corporation, which is common for individual with a high net worth. Given that he purchases and sells shares of many companies, the use of a limited liability company (LLC) allows him to decide when to take money out of the company, without paying taxes on any gains until he decides to remove funds from the firm. The result is controlling how much has to be spent each year in income taxes while also maintaining business interests and building funds that can be distributed later as part of his pledge to donate the vast majority of his net worth during his life (or within 20 years of the passing of the last surviving spouse).

CASCADE INVESTMENT, LLC

Bill Gates's investments outside of Microsoft, the Bill and Melinda Gates Foundation, and Corbis are held under the name Cascade Investment, LLC. As a private corporation, many of his holdings do not need to be reported under applicable law. However, information can be ascertained about the types of organizations Gates invests in through regulatory filings (when required) as well as news releases. His chief investment officer is Michael Larson, who has held that position since 1994. In corporations where Gates holds more than 10 percent of the company, Larson often represents his interests on the board of directors.

Gates owns 47.5 percent of the company Four Seasons Hotel Inc., the Four Seasons brand name, and the property management division. During the last three months of 2013, he also bought three hotels using the Four Seasons brand. In September 2013, he bought the Four Seasons Houston for approximately $140 million, October saw him acquire the Four Seasons Atlanta for $62 million, and December saw him purchase the Four Seasons Resort Punta Mita—near Puerto Vallarta, Mexico—for $200 million.[12]

Gates owns over 16 million shares of the car dealership firm AutoNation, and Larson serves as the chair of the committee that determines executive compensation. Gates, much like his good friend Warren Buffett, also shows an interest in innovative firms that are in industries that are considered low-tech. For instance, Gates owns just under 90 million shares of Republic Services, which deals with waste and recycling, far eclipsing the next largest shareholder with fewer than 14 million shares. There Larson currently serves as the chairperson of the committee that nominates new directors and reviews corporate governance. Gates owns almost 28 million shares of EcoLab, which is largely known as a food, water, and environmental safety firm, yet holds over 5,300 patents, inventing new products at a high rate. Larson represents Gates's major shareholding by serving on two committees of the board of directors.[13]

Berkshire Hathaway, the company controlled by Warren Buffett, bought all of Burlington Northern Santa Fe (BNSF) railroad, and that form of investment apparently appealed to Gates, who purchased over 43 million shares of the Canadian National (CN) railroad, and is the largest single shareholder. He also purchased more than 8 percent of Deere and Co, known for the John Deere products seen on lawns, farms, and construction sites. Bill Gates bought almost 6 percent of Spanish construction company FCC (Fomento de Constucciones & Contratas), in the belief that the Spanish economy was recovering in October 2013.[14]

And Gates also invests directly with his friend Warren Buffett. "Cascade, which the billionaire solely owns, also controls 4,350 Class A shares of Omaha, Nebraska-based Berkshire Hathaway Inc." While that does not sound like many shares compared to Microsoft or other firms where Gates owns millions of shares, each Class A share of Berkshire Hathaway was worth $177,900 when the year 2013 ended; his shares of Berkshire Hathaway alone were worth over $750 million.[15]

CORBIS

The initial company founded by Gates is now called Corbis but was originally called Interactive Home Systems. At the time of founding in 1989, Gates made a slight miscalculation in his belief that individuals would want to purchase images that could be used and projected in the home, like on television sets.

The firm continues Gates's belief in intellectual capital, as all of the products sold by Corbis are images, videos, or the rights to use the visual likeness of various celebrities, musicians, and movies. Like software, the items being licensed are not anything that has to be created multiple times for use. For instance a photograph created once can be relicensed multiple times with little additional cost, especially when purchases can all be conducted online. Each additional license thus has very little in terms of marginal cost to the firm, which means profit can exist on each additional sale despite low sales costs.

Gary Shenk is the CEO of Corbis, and Bill Gates is the chairman of the firm, much like the arrangement at Microsoft had been when Bill Gates continued to serve as executive chairman while Steve Ballmer served as CEO until the appointment of Satya Nadella as the new CEO in February 2014 (when Gates decided to undertake a mentoring role instead).

Within the Corbis organization, there are a total of four subsidiaries that provide services to distinct customer segments. Corbis Images

Bill Gates speaks at the 2006 Corbis annual meeting. Corbis and subsidiary firms are wholly owned by Gates. (AP Photo/Bebeto Matthews)

focuses on the sale of still photographs, while Corbis Motion focuses on videos, including aerial videos of cities and landscapes. For instance, an individual can purchase and license the use of photographs of Bill Gates through Corbis Images. The intellectual property of celebrity marketing, existing movies, and music is controlled by Corbis Entertainment, which also uses the name Green Light Rights. For instance, any use of images for Albert Einstein, Charlie Chaplin, Dr. Martin Luther King Jr., and Steve McQueen would require authorization from a company controlled by Bill Gates. Another subsidiary is called Veer, which sells artistic photos and specialized fonts for computer users, usually the lower-cost items sold by the organization. Then there is Splash News, which specializes in current photos, news, and stories related to celebrities and individuals involved with popular culture.

According to Corbis's fact sheet, the company has approximately 650 employees and customers in more than 50 countries as of January 1, 2014. The library of images available from Corbis represents the work of more than 30,000 photographers around the world, all searchable online for quick and easy purchasing by businesses and organizations desiring to use those photos.[16]

Corbis was not always a profitable company and required restructuring at one point in time. In an interview with CEO Shenk, there were three primary issues that confronted the company in the 2006/2007 timeframe. As has been seen in other industries like photography, there was a rapid shift from print photographs to digital. In addition, more capable devices like cell phones and tablets were able to take and display digital photographs. Finally, the creation of photographs by millions of individuals around the world created a market where low-cost—or free—options were readily available when Corbis had specialized in higher-cost options that started at $150 and ranged to $500.

The issue of providing high-cost options when lower-cost options were becoming prevalent was compounded by the global recession that started shortly thereafter. Fortunately, Bill Gates saw the need to re-envision the company once again, from a company that was oriented toward digital media on televisions to specialized media rights to providing a full range of licensing that includes low-cost as well as high-cost options, for individuals and professionals.[17]

Lawsuit against Corbis

Corbis was sued in a fraud case for stealing the intellectual property of a firm called InfoFlows. The most recent public documents about the case suggest that the Washington State Court of Appeals ruled that Corbis would be required to pay $12.75 million in damages to Info-Flows. This was a number reduced from an original $36 million in damages. Based upon the initial claim, the reaffirmation of the fine against Corbis would suggest that intellectual property of InfoFlows was used to create a patent application for Corbis:

> According to the claim by Infoflows, Corbis abruptly terminated the contract after four months and claimed ownership of the technology. Infoflows then discovered that Corbis was patenting its own system based on what Infoflows saw as its own IP. In January 2007, Corbis sued Infoflows for breach of contract and trade secret misappropriation. Infoflows countersued claiming several charges of fraud.[18]

Chapter 11

BILL AND MELINDA GATES FOUNDATION AND GIVING PLEDGE

The couple founded what is now the largest independent charitable foundation in the world, committing to dispersing the vast majority of their accumulated wealth. Beginning with his departure from Microsoft in 2008, Gates has declared his work with the Bill and Melinda Gates Foundation to be his full-time work.

Bill Gates recognized the importance of being involved in social causes as his mother had been throughout his upbringing until her death in 1994. However, he was very clear that the social involvement was not being driven by a requirement from his mother. In fact, Gates finds exceptional personal reward and satisfaction in the ability to contribute to solving problems with the resources he had amassed.

PRECEDENTS FOR MASSIVE GIVING

Gates, Allen, Ballmer, and Jobs all became exceptionally wealthy as part of the micro-computer revolution. In terms of philanthropy, Gates did have role models from other individuals who had amassed incredible amounts of wealth through previous revolutions in business, like another cluster of famous names—John D. Rockefeller, Andrew Carnegie, and John Pierpont (J.P.) Morgan, all born between 1835 and 1839.

How did John D. Rockefeller give? He gave primarily to educational institutions throughout the country, benefiting others who had often been neglected, like providing funding to help found Spelman College—a school founded in the 19th century to educate African American women in Atlanta—as well as initiatives to help promote public health, including efforts to eradicate hookworm.

How did Andrew Carnegie give? He worked in education as well, specifically in libraries. At one point in U.S. history, Carnegie had paid for the construction of almost half of the libraries in the entire country, so his initiative provided access. The Carnegie Mellon University is a combination of the university he founded and Mellon Institute; he also provided funds to the Tuskegee Institute to support African American education. He provided funding for science and research, and supported the arts through Carnegie Hall.

How did J.P. Morgan give? He gave to colleges, universities, and museums, and the items he collected throughout life were used as educational tools and museum pieces.

So Gates had many potential models to follow—he could use his expertise in technology to benefit education, work with libraries, support higher education, help African Americans and other disadvantaged populations build better lives, work on health initiatives, promote new scientific approaches, or use items collected for educational tools as museum pieces, as Rockefeller, Carnegie, and Morgan had a century before. Or with an exceptionally focused mind and desire to benefit the most people and save lives at the lowest cost, Gates's philanthropy could very well assist in completing all mentioned earlier. However, Gates did not start his philanthropy—or collecting—with such a broad focus.

GATES AND LEONARDO DaVINCI

What do Bill Gates and Leonardo DaVinci have in common aside from an ability to see connections and opportunities where others could not? Gates bought one of DaVinci's scientific journals, called the *Codex Leicester*, in 1994 for $30,802,500 at a Christie's art auction. Why does this one document sell for such a high price? No other work created by DaVinci is owned by a person—all other known documents are owned by governments or museums. But what does one do when owning a work created over 600 years ago by one of the greatest inventors in all of history?

Gates used the product in his digital imaging company (Corbis) but also wanted to share it with the world, allowing others to view the important document. There was a minor problem along the way, and Gates decided to "test out" the implications of acquiring other expensive artworks and pieces of historical significance over time. Buying an item in New York for over $30 million was still an expensive purchase despite his wealth, and Gates understood that as a resident of Washington State, he was supposed to pay taxes on the item purchased in another state at the time he brought the item to Washington.

In 1995, Bill called someone at his father's law firm to try to get a new law passed, working with an official in the state's Department of Revenue, who recalled later:

> If Bill Gates had to pay nearly $3 million to bring the da Vinci manuscript into this state, why would he? He has eight or nine homes. He can leave it in a state without paying a use tax. I thought applying the use tax to art collectors would result in someone either not bringing (the art) into the state or not purchasing it at all. I saw it as my job to help draft the legislation so that it was specific and didn't include more (exemptions) than intended.[1]

The law never passed, as there were some objections. Other collectors of valuable items in the state of Washington were apparently not paying the required tax, and the proposed bill quietly went away (until published in the news 10 years later). The reporter noted that Gates paid the legally required tax to bring the valuable into the state, and allowed the document to have public showings in the local community—the Seattle Art Museum in 1997 and the Boeing Museum of Flight in 2006—and around the world. Coincidentally, Bill Gates's father had married the director of the Seattle Art Museum (Mimi Gardner) in 1996.

LIBRARY PROJECT AND U.S. INITIATIVE

The first major project was the Library Project in the United States, from 1996 to 2003, with the primary years from 1998 to 2003. The focus was on providing access to computers and training in U.S. and Canadian public libraries, primarily in poor and rural areas. This single project was valued at almost $180 million: "We funded training and the initial hardware grants, and Microsoft provided some of the software that people used, but the connectivity piece is ongoing."[2]

Using the Internet to communicate with families and looking for jobs was expected; searching for information about medical issues like those soon to be funded by Gates Foundation jumped out. The project covered almost 11,000 facilities with over 47,000 computers and 62,000 opportunities for training. At the time of the grant, the Internet was not available to everyone and the goal of the project was to allow anyone who went to a library to have Internet access, that objective was only 95 percent achieved by Gates's estimation.

Gates expected criticism that providing Microsoft products would be seen as attracting new customers but Gates saw this as a have-versus-have-not issue in society: how to allow people without computers or access to the Internet to benefit from the tool. Gates did not expect criticism like he received from the *New York Times*, suggesting that a goal of connecting people in rural areas was to encourage movement away from the rural areas.

In his clear vision of the future regarding books and computers, he described how the *Wall Street Journal* was at 75 percent paper and 25 percent computer-based for reading but "eventually these computer screens are going to get small and portable." In 2003, Gates already saw the future for devices like Amazon's Kindle, Apple's iPad, Barnes & Noble's Nook, and the tablets of various other manufacturers in revolutionizing the way books could be read, from entirely paper-based to electronic.[3]

Others glommed on to the library project with comparisons to Carnegie, who paid for the library construction but required the community to provide the books and resources. Martin wrote that it would be common and expected for technology magnates to donate technology to libraries, that the patrons with no other Internet access would benefit, and that there was a necessary role with instruction of these new resources; although not directly manipulating these individuals without Internet access, it was seen as a form of marketing toward these same groups.[4]

WEALTH DISPARITY AND MINORITY EDUCATION

In 1997, the JBHE foundation wrote that 7.2 percent of gifts made by Bill Gates at that time were directed explicitly toward historically black colleges and universities (HBCUs). Gates had not ramped up massive amounts of donations at the time, but the authors stated that if all future giving by Gates continued at the existing levels, the amount donated—in 1997 dollars—would be at least three times the then value of the endowments at all private black colleges combined. The authors noted that Gates had made a point to intentionally reach out to those colleges and universities, and that a small percentage of Gates's wealth would make a profound impact on those colleges and universities.[5]

Two years later in the same *JBHE* journal, Cross wrote that Bill and Melinda Gates Foundation gave $1 billion to be administered primarily by the United Negro College Fund (UNCF) under the Gates Millennium Scholarship Fund Endowment, specifically to provide funding for low-income minorities to seek college education. On average, Cross found that minority families are shown by the Census Bureau to have approximately one-tenth the family wealth of Caucasian families, which precludes some minority students from seeking college studies. However, there were concerns about the use of funds to provide opportunities only to poor minority students, despite the source being a private endowment instead of a government agency.[6] The Gates Millennium Scholarship Fund program remains open to African American, American Indian—Alaska Native, Asian Pacific Islander American, and Hispanic American students.[7]

A billion dollars to education is a very large number, but a billion dollars would be a small percentage of Bill Gates net worth. Two years later in 2001, the *JBHE*, extrapolating from 1995 U.S. Census Bureau data, estimated that Bill Gates alone held almost 10 times as much wealth in just Microsoft stock than the entire wealth of all African American households in the U.S. *combined*. Gates had decided to give away the vast majority of his wealth, but others continued to notice that there was inequity given Gates's vast comparative wealth compared to others in his own country, no less abroad.[8] Despite his commitment to giving away his wealth and two in-progress initiatives, Gates drew heat from an unlikely source: consumer advocate Ralph Nader.

1998 EDUCATION SPEECH PIEING INCIDENT

In February 1998, Bill Gates was due to give a speech on education in Brussels, Belgium, when he was hit in the face with four small pies.

The two pie throwers were fined approximately $88 each the next year, the minimum allowed under Belgian law for the crime of "mild violence." Even though Gates was in Belgium to talk about an important issue, he was specifically one of many individuals targeted by the group of pie throwers: "The group's mastermind, Noel Godin, has vowed to 'assassinate through ridicule all world celebrities who take themselves spectacularly seriously.'"[9]

RALPH NADER'S ACTIVISM IN 1998

How is Ralph Nader connected to Bill Gates, Warren Buffett, the current mission of the Bill and Melinda Gates Foundation, and the Giving Pledge later initiated by Gates and Buffett? That story starts back in 1998, when Nader was pressing Gates on multiple issues, including those that led to the Microsoft trial. Therefore, on July 27, 1998, Nader sent Gates a letter starting with a sobering figure about Gates's wealth at that time: according to a study by an economist, Gates alone was reportedly wealthier than the poorest 40 percent of Americans *combined*.

Nader took those mathematical figures a bit further, discerning that the wealth of the 385 billionaires in the world at the time exceeded the wealth of the poorest 3 billion people on the earth (that is 3,000,000,000 people). So Nader had a few thoughts about what these exceptionally wealthy people could do to assist others throughout the globe.

He describes the deaths that occur globally due to diseases that are rare in the United States because medical treatment is effective and inexpensive, yet not acted upon by businesses or governments in any coordinated fashion. He even noted that deaths from tuberculosis and malaria were increasing, with a record of almost 6 million people dying in the previous calendar year. Nader knew, from Gates's writing, speeches, and events, that Gates and Warren Buffett, two of the top-three wealthiest people in the world, were very good friends. As a result, he made a prescriptive recommendation that Gates and Buffett create a billionaire summit that would use the expertise and resources of these successful businesspersons to solve problems throughout the world by initiating a:

[C]onference of billionaires and multi-billionaires on the subject of National and Global Wealth Disparities and What to Do

About It. The quantity, quality and distributional dimensions of economic output will drive participants to come to grips with the fundamental purposes of economic systems and their economic indicators.[10]

Did Bill Gates respond to Nader's letter? He did indeed on August 4, mentioning his already existing commitment to give away the vast majority of his wealth in his lifetime and that he has to protect his wealth—by effectively running Microsoft—in order to provide the most social good in the future. He also subtly made a jab at himself and/or Nader, specifying that experts in one area should not make recommendations in areas where expertise is lacking: "I am in agreement with my friend, Warren Buffett, when he says that people who are successful in one field should be careful about suggesting they know all the answers in other areas."[11]

Gates knew that technology did provide societal improvements in terms of education and personal health, which he had seen with his library project in the United States. For instance, people used the access to the Internet for communication but also to research medical issues and diagnoses. Gates also used technological advancements and improvements as the theme of both books he authored. He also provided a subtle comment about using success in one aspect in life to infer expertise in other spheres. This statement could be interpreted as applying to each of the three parties (Gates's expertise was technology/business, Buffett's expertise was investing, and Nader's expertise was consumer activism); none were experts in driving initiatives that were intended to drive broad societal improvements.

Nader used Gates's letter as an opportunity to release one more statement, responding that he was not calling into question the philanthropic efforts of Gates, simply asking that those most wealthy meet to speak about issues that might be solved given attention to inequality of wealth. Nader also mentioned speaking to two other exceptionally wealthy individuals, who believed his proposal had merit.[12] If those two individuals—Ted Turner (known for variously owning CNN, TBS, the Atlanta Braves, and being the largest landowner in the United States) and Sol Price (whose Price Club stores eventually became part of the current Costco chain)—were both believers in billionaires addressing this problem, why would Nader be insistent that Gates alone be the one who initiated the conference? Nader had initiated a critical attack on Microsoft the previous year, leading to a November 1997 conference he called *Appraising Microsoft and Its Global Strategy*; Gates referenced this Nader-initiated conference at the November 1997 Microsoft Shareholder Meeting. Nader had—conveniently—scheduled his conference for the same day as Microsoft's Shareholder Meeting, so there was little chance Gates or other senior executives would have attended even if interested in the offer. The Microsoft Shareholder Meeting had been announced the week before Nader's request for Gates's attendance.

While Gates personally never responded to Nader's invitation, his organization did through Microsoft executive vice president and chief operating officer Bob Herbold in a letter, objecting that Nader's organization would not provide an opportunity for meaningful discourse with sessions led entirely by Microsoft critics, competitors, and those suing Microsoft. The entire proceedings were compared to a kangaroo court as Microsoft's recommendations for panelists were rejected. Herbold ended by noting that due to the computing revolution, the access, speed, and cost of computing had decreased so dramatically that other major industries would not be able to maintain the same pace of increasing value to the consumer:

> Your premise that Microsoft has been a disincentive to competition and innovation is simply wrong. As an AT&T executive observed last year, the cost of computing has fallen 10 million-fold since the microprocessor was invented in 1971. That's the equivalent of getting a Boeing 747 for the price of a pizza. If this innovation had been applied to automotive technology, a new car would cost about $2; it would travel at the speed of sound; and it would go 600 miles on a thimble of gas.[13]

Herbold incorporates a statement made by Michael Rothschild (the "AT&T executive") that supports the claims made by Gates, Microsoft, and others in the technology industry. The increases in capability and widespread adoption in a period of just under 25 years had put—in almost every U.S. home—computing products that were far superior in capability than even the largest computers available to the biggest corporations at the beginning of the 1970s, at costs most families could afford.

As relayed by Clausing in the next day's *New York Times*, Microsoft's concerns of an *in absentia* round of bashing by the company's opponents was well supported. And Microsoft executives, of course, were at the Microsoft shareholder meeting.

> Scott McNealy, the chief executive of Sun Microsystems, gave the keynote address, telling the audience he was the only competitor left able to publicly talk against Microsoft because he is the only one with an alternative operating system to Windows, Java . . . "It's about standards on the Web," McNealy said. "Very few people are willing to stand up to the power of Microsoft. Some people think Sun is committing corporate suicide by not reselling Microsoft. I just think it's Web suicide if we don't have choice."[14]

NADER, GATES, AND PHILANTHROPY

Given the low-quality interactions between Gates and Nader, there was little chance Gates would immediately convene a summit of billionaires (with the help of Warren Buffett) that would lead to philanthropic efforts to solve problems globally, including health initiatives that could save lives without much funding. Given some time—a decade or so—Gates and Buffett do lead an initiative involving the world's billionaires in philanthropy, and Gates begins to focus on health initiatives that did save lives.

In fact, that disparity in wealth has increased since the time of Nader's original letter, despite the involvement of many nonprofit organizations and the initiatives led by Gates and other billionaires. Oxfam used information presented in Credit Suisse's "2013 Global Wealth Report" to estimate that the wealthiest 85 people in the world then controlled as much as the bottom 50 percent of the global population (3.5 billion people); the 1998 figure was 385 richest people controlling as much wealth as the poorest 3 billion people.[15]

STARTING THE FOUNDATION

Gates's father was quoted on the struggle to get him to develop a Foundation to benefit others. In fact, Gates himself—in his letter to Nader—had stressed that his current project was to work to make

Microsoft successful such that there would be more funds available for philanthropy later. And with the focus on Microsoft's success:

> "He regarded it," his father Bill Gates Sr., noted "as another management problem which would intrude on his time, which was his most precious commodity and so he had uniformly repelled the idea of starting a foundation.". . .
>
> "He thought the most important thing to do," his father said, "was to have the business succeed." The young entrepreneur told his mother that philanthropy was fine, but he had to pay his employees, to drum up enough business; after all, it was a very competitive market out there. Eventually, young Gates came around, putting a United Way campaign in place at Microsoft. "So," his father said, "his instincts for philanthropy were there."[16]

When did the idea for the Foundation actually coalesce and take off? While in line for a a movie, an idea came up that perhaps Bill himself would not have to run the Foundation on a day-to-day basis. And his father volunteered assistance. Bill Gates Sr. then says, "My son decided maybe it was time to start a foundation." What had changed Bill's mind? "I think it was the revelation that maybe there was somebody available to take the responsibility for managing [the foundation]."[17]

FOUNDATION AND AIMS

Between 20 and 25 percent of all funded projects are made in the United States, under a belief system that every life has equal value, regardless of location in the world.[18] Bill and Melinda Gates are co-chairs along with his father, William H. Gates Sr., and close friend Warren Buffett is a trustee. According to the organization's fact sheet, the Foundation has over 1,000 staff members, over $40 billion in the current trust account, and had made $28.3 billion in grants since founding, with work in over 100 countries, all U.S. states, and Washington, D.C.

As Gates mentioned in the earliest days of Microsoft, he could negotiate business deals without the assistance of lobbyists; in the role of the Gates Foundation, he and his wife have important roles as leaders and policymakers, frequently speaking to raise awareness of initiatives.

*Bill and Melinda Gates with a
tuberculosis patient in Cape Town,
South Africa, in July 2006.
(AP Photo/Bill & Melinda Gates
Foundation, Sharon Farmer)*

Among the largest committed grants are the GAVI Alliance for childhood vaccinations, the Gates Millennium Scholars Program, the U.S., efforts on malaria vaccines, and a contribution to Rotary International's PolioPlus initiative, which seeks to eliminate the disease polio throughout the world. And Gates is results-oriented; efforts like eradicating polio has led to just three countries in the world still having the disease as of January 2014 (and reduction in worldwide polio cases by 99% in the past 35 years).

LETTER FROM BILL AND MELINDA GATES

In their letter announcing the aims of the Foundation, the family does talk about focusing on a limited number of goals, where the greatest impacts can be made (both in saving lives and allowing individuals to make the most of their lives): "Our friend and co-trustee Warren Buffett once gave us some great advice about philanthropy: 'Don't just go for safe projects,' he said. 'Take on the really tough problems.'"[19]

CHANGING THE MISSION

Early in the days of the Foundation, the focus was on library projects in the United States and providing educational opportunities for students of impoverished financial backgrounds. Later, in an interview with Bill Moyers, Gates spoke about why initiatives outside the United States would become the primary focus, as he saw evidence of many people dying from issues that were not only preventable, but the investment required to make a difference in the lives of millions would be fairly inexpensive in the scope of the Foundation, as long as a well-reasoned approach was taken. While reading a report, he found that people around the world were still dying of mosquito-borne disease and lack of vaccinations, which were not problems encountered in the United States:

> I know when I saw that article on the World Development Report, I said, this can't be true, but if it is true, this deserves to be the priority of our giving. And so I took the article and Melinda read it. I gave it to my dad and said, you know can you have the people you're working with, tell me is this some aberration here? Or if this is true, give me more things to read.
>
> It was a shock, but then, you know it was an answer to say that governments weren't doing it.
>
> And so maybe we could help step in. And maybe not just our resources, but maybe we could galvanize some interest and attention and IQ to go and look at these problems and think you know if I have the technology that can you know stop mosquitoes from carrying these diseases. Or allow vaccines to be delivered without a refrigerator, you know I have saved millions of lives by coming up with those ideas.[20]

The Gates family recognized immediately that with the exceptional amount of financial resources allocated to improving the lives of others through the Bill and Melinda Gates Foundation, some of the most effective options could come at comparatively low cost. Rather than focus on rare diseases that are costly to treat and only saving a few lives, the Gates Foundation takes a very strategic approach. Gates still provides insight into his very analytical mind, thinking about diseases that cause the greatest number of deaths throughout the world, how many lives can be saved, and the meaningful improvement that comes based upon the involvement of the Bill and Melinda Gates Foundation.

In 2001, Kickbusch[21] wrote, "In the short period of three years your Bill and Melinda Gates Foundation has supported global health development in your areas of choice (vaccine development and maternal and child health). The budget of the World Health Organisation pales in comparison. You should be praised for this commitment." She suggested that philanthropy often gets stuck with unintended consequences, where various entities are attempting to raise funds for the same causes, effectively getting in each other's way. She appeals to Gates's business acumen and says, "The next big challenge for global health is not yet another disease initiative. John Maynard Keynes helped invent the United Nations. Bill, go the next step and invest your creativity, resources and influence to help create a financially viable network structure fit for global public health in the 21st century."[22]

The Gates Foundation continued its focus of saving the most lives and causing the most improvement, not the amount of dollars given. And for a disease like malaria, which infects and kills millions of people throughout the world each year, grants Gates felt to be small were actually exceptionally large in a global context, saving many lives with comparatively few funds. And given the approach the Foundation takes when working to solve problems, Gates himself was shocked upon discovering that life-saving work could easily be done—that others had not already adopted or championed the causes that impact so many people throughout the world.

> You think in philanthropy that your dollars will just be marginal, because the really juicy obvious things will all have been taken. So you look at this stuff and we are, like, wow! When somebody is saying to you we can save many lives for hundreds of dollars each, the answer has to be no, no, no. That would already have been done.[23]

In speeches on important days in his life, as when Harvard bestowed upon him an honorary doctoral degree, he spoke about the mission of the Foundation, how every life has value, and stressed that the most important advances and the highest possible achievements made are those that reduce inequity around the world.

But humanity's greatest advances are not in its discoveries—but in how those discoveries are applied to reduce inequity. Whether through democracy, strong public education, quality health care, or broad economic opportunity—reducing inequity is the highest human achievement.

If you believe that every life has equal value, it's revolting to learn that some lives are seen as worth saving and others are not. We said to ourselves: "This can't be true. But if it is true, it deserves to be the priority of our giving."[24]

DAVOS, 2008 WORLD ECONOMIC FORUM

At the 2008 World Economic Forum Conference in Davos, Switzerland, Gates gave a talk called *Creative Capitalism*. This later became a book, including the contributions of Bill Gates and Warren Buffett among others: "The world is getting better, but it's not getting better fast enough, and it's not getting better for everyone."[25]

INFLECTION POINT

Davos was an inflection point for Bill Gates, for he was about to leave his full-time work at Microsoft. Although he had, somewhat reluctantly, left the CEO position back in 2000, he had remained involved with the company he cofounded for an additional eight years in multiple roles. By 2008, Gates had been with Microsoft since day one and was the only person remaining who had seen the first eight years of the firm. The only other person who had experienced the first eight years of the firm had been Paul Allen, who commented on the impending departure of Gates: "It may be more of a change than he thinks," says Paul Allen, recalling his own departure from Microsoft in 1983. "You don't always realize how dramatic that transition is going to be when people aren't depending on your decisions day by day."[26]

Toward the end of his day-to-day role at Microsoft, Gates acknowledged the statement by Allen and said that switching from Microsoft would be an "adjustment": "So, yeah, I have an adjustment to make. I've done the same thing for 33 years, in a sense. . . . It will be an adjustment for me. If I didn't have the foundation—which is so exciting, and the work is complex—if I didn't have that, it would be tough for me, because I'm not a sit-on-the-beach type."[27]

He also recognized that not only did he want to do good work, but that if he were to stay with Microsoft as long as there were challenges from competitors, full-time work with the Foundation could never happen. In fact, he would have to work until his last day on earth, and didn't see devoting all of his efforts to the Foundation to be giving up something he valued the past 33 years of his life, but as a new—and fun—activity.

If you say, "Gosh, I won't leave when there's an interesting competitor," then you'd have to die on the job.

I love the fact that I get to meet with scientists who are devoting their lives to these things. So in no sense would I say, "Oh, I'm making a sacrifice to do something my mother told me I ought to do." I *am* doing something my mother told me I ought to do, but I'm doing it because it's going to be a lot of fun.[28]

Gates knew he had amassed financial wealth, and had his own view of what should happen to massive wealth if still present at the death of the wealth-holder. Sharing the same view as his father, Gates strongly believed that if a person earning the wealth didn't give those funds away—in his or her lifetime or through a charitable foundation—that the funds should be subjected to estate taxes before being passed to any heirs. Of course, Gates had long committed to ensuring that the majority of his wealth would be used to improve the lives of others through the Bill and Melinda Gates Foundation. He also recognized that his success was based not just on his own achievement but the educational system afforded to him as well as other benefits that can be attributed to government intervention, such as a stable country where rights and freedoms to create his company were present: "And my case is a clear one. I'm a beneficiary of an educational system and a system of stability and incentives, where I got to hire bright people and come up with products. And the fact I was 19 years old, that didn't matter. If I had a good piece of software, somebody could buy it from me."[29]

EVER THE INNOVATOR

Just ask Bill Gates. If he were a teenager again, he'd be biology hacking. "Creating artificial life with DNA synthesis. That's sort of the equivalent of machine language programming," says Gates, whose work for the Bill and Melinda Gates Foundation has led him to become a didactic expert in disease and immunology. "If you want to change the world in some big way, that's where you should start—biological molecules. Those are all pretty deep problems that need the same type of crazy fanaticism and youthful genius and naiveté that drove the PC industry, and can have the same impact on the human condition.[30]

Gates readily saw that the charitable causes that attracted funding were those that were prevalent in more affluent countries. The individuals who lived in poorer countries, where easy to treat diseases were endemic, faced undue suffering and deaths that were preventable. Medical conditions such as baldness are exceptionally minor in comparison: "This leads to the paradox, that because the disease is only in the poor countries, there is not much investment. For example, there is more money put into baldness drugs than are put into malaria. Now baldness is a terrible thing (laughter). And rich men are afflicted, so that is why that priority is set."[31]

Bill Gates is not the only member of the household with a critical role in the Bill and Melinda Gates Foundation. His wife Melinda would be his third major partner in Eisner's narrative; she is also a visionary and conversant on the issues the Foundation seeks to address, leading efforts in initiatives such as reproductive health. Despite her broad influence in the Foundation, many observers do not see her role:

> They think he's doing it all, and that's okay. That is just the state of affairs. But I think as soon as they start to hear me talk about the issues and talk about what's real and why we're doing it, they start to realize, "Oh, okay, we get it. This is a partnership."[32]

In 2011, Gates declared that despite his great wealth and contributions from others like Warren Buffett, that the Foundation was created to end within two decades of the passing of Bill and Melinda: "Our foundation won't last long beyond Melinda's and my lifetime. The resources will last about 20 years after whichever is the last of us to go. There is no family business, and my kids will make their own careers."[33]

RE-ENVISIONING THE TOILET

Along with the low-cost initiatives that save lives, Gates has also worked with organizations to other initiatives that require creative thinking to save lives. In 2014, one of those initiatives was the "Reinvent the Toilet Challenge," which he presented to the National Academy of Sciences—leading experts and many Nobel Prize winners—at a 150th anniversary event. The expertise of these individuals would help derive with new ideas to solve challenges that are often not contemplated in more affluent regions. The toilets most of us recognize are still not available to 40 percent of the world's population and require infrastructure—water and sewer services—that are unavailable or unaffordable. As a result, 1.5 million children a year die from contaminated water supplies.

Gates mentioned awarding three prizes to teams of students from universities in the first *Reinvent the Toilet Challenge*, even joking by writing "It probably says something about me that I really had fun handing out prizes for toilet designs."[34]

CRITICISM OF VACCINES, EDUCATIONAL INITIATIVES, AND SCOPE

On the Internet, one can readily find various sites with identical statements to suggest that the vaccines created with the support of the Bill and Melinda Gates Foundation are intended to reduce the population and/or cause widespread harm to children. Fortunately, these sites are untrue; however, the belief of a link between the vaccines and afflictions like autism has prevented many children from receiving ordinary vaccinations. In an interview with Dr. Sanjay Gupta of CNN, Gates spoke about the discredited research:

(Sanjay) Gupta: There has been a lot of scrutiny of vaccines recently—specifically childhood vaccines. There has been a lot of news about is there a connection with autism, for example.

What do you make of all that? Dr. [Andrew] Wakefield wrote a paper about this [in The Lancet in 1998] saying he thought there was a connection. And there were lower vaccination rates over a period of time as a result in Britain, then the United States. What are your thoughts?

(Bill) Gates: Well, Dr. Wakefield has been shown to have used absolutely fraudulent data. He had a financial interest in some law-suits, he created a fake paper, the journal allowed it to run. All the other studies were done, showed no connection whatsoever again and again and again. So it's an absolute lie that has killed thousands of kids. Because the mothers who heard that lie, many of them didn't have their kids take either pertussis or measles vaccine, and their children are dead today. And so the people who go and en-gage in those anti-vaccine efforts—you know, they, they kill chil-dren. It's a very sad thing, because these vaccines are important.[35]

The article where the researcher claimed to make the link between vaccines and disease was indeed retracted (taken back as incorrect) by the publisher; an investigation showed that the research was paid for by parents who wanted to sue vaccine makers, that he conducted medical tests without ethical permission, and that he had patented a different vaccine for profit (one that would be used if the one he wrote about negatively was taken off the market).[36]

In education, the Foundation was subject to criticism for the Gates Millennium Scholarship Fund for minority students seeking college study, driven by his awareness that students with minority backgrounds were far less likely to be able to afford college. With K-12 education, the criticism is centered on topics such as the Gates Foundation paying for the development of the Common Core Educational Standards in the United States—effectively, the Foundation creates an idea of what should be taught instead of the government doing so.[37] Furthermore, the Foundation did not accurately interpret statistics before providing grants to support smaller schools, then not seeing the desired impact. A third initiative subject to criticism has been using a private sector tool of ranking teachers, partially based upon educational attainment of the students, to decide which teachers should be more highly compensated and which should not be retained.[38]

In response to a question about criticism the Foundation receives about changing behavior due to the size and scope of the Foundation, Gates acknowledges that controversy is a part of tackling the problems. With educational institutions in particular, he notes that charter schools are one way of testing the theories he proposes for success or failure, and that the government is the largest actor in the field of education.

When we get into a field, we do take a point of view, and raising controversy is a symptom. Fortunately, there is what's called the charter school format that lets you try new things. The system is good at shutting down the ones that don't work and replicating the ones that do. The big actor is government. If somebody says somebody is too big, it would be strange to point to us.[39]

2014 ANNUAL LETTER

In 2014, Bill and Melinda Gates released their annual letter on behalf of their Foundation, a practice he had picked up from his friend Warren Buffett, who issues an annual letter to Berkshire Hathaway shareholders. In that document, he made a sweeping new prediction: "I am optimistic enough about this that I am willing to make a prediction. By 2035, there will be almost no poor countries left in the world. Almost all countries will be what we now call lower-middle income or richer."[40]

Combined, Bill and Melinda made a conscious effort to refute three of the myths that they felt were constraining success in the fights against poverty and disease, with data they hoped could be shared in discussions at all levels.

Myth 1: Poor countries are doomed to stay poor.
Myth 2: Aid is wasted.
Myth 3: Saving lives leads to overpopulation.

In a compelling way, Bill dispelled the first two myths with data showing increases in global wealth and stressed that in cases where people believe aid is wasted, the results-driven experience he has with the Gates Foundation actually reveals the limited cases of abuse while the vast majority of pledged aid is truly doing well. Melinda provides data to refute claims that saving lives leads to overpopulation, with evidence that families have fewer children as infant mortality decreases.[41]

THE GIVING PLEDGE

Once a vast quantity of wealth is amassed, the holder of that wealth faces many choices. There are no government regulations restricting the maximum wealth of an individual, provided compliance with appropriate tax laws. A wealthy person has many options ranging from maintaining the wealth and passing to future generations of family or associates, using the wealth to fund major endeavors during his or her lifetime, or using some/all of the wealth to pursue philanthropic pursuits.

In 2010, Bill and Melinda Gates teamed with Warren Buffett, challenging the wealthiest U.S. residents to commit at least half of the accumulated wealth toward philanthropic initiatives: "We have been blessed with good fortune beyond our wildest expectations, and we are profoundly grateful. But just as these gifts are great, so we feel a great responsibility to use them well. That is why we are so pleased to join in making an explicit commitment to the Giving Pledge."[42]

Due to the wealth amassed through Microsoft and various other initiatives, the Gates family recognized that personal family needs could be met with only a small proportion of those assets. However, the Gates family and Warren Buffett are exceptionally influential people, who have the ability to speak to other billionaires who might have the same interest in promoting philanthropy or charitable causes. Consumer advocate Ralph Nader had realized the influence of these two individuals in 1998 but was a bit of an antagonist to Gates and Microsoft at the time. From the connections made by Gates and Buffett, the idea of the Giving Pledge was initiated.

The Giving Pledge is not any form of contract that requires billionaires to use funds for philanthropy or charitable causes; the pledge itself is merely a public statement that more than half of the wealth would be used to support this form of cause within their lifetime (or willed at the time of their deaths). The pledge originally started with U.S. billionaires or those whose wealth plus previous donations exceeded a billion dollars. While a small group of U.S. citizens, these individuals and families have the potential resources to make powerful differences in improving the life of others, and the hope is that these public commitments from the wealthiest people in the United States will encourage more individuals to similarly become involved in philanthropy and charities, not just now but for many generations into the future.

Of particular note is that the Giving Pledge is entirely separate from the Bill & Melinda Gates Foundation or any other charity, foundation, or organization. Each individual or family member making the pledge maintains complete control over how his or her pledge will be used to improve the world, and the Gates family asks for no contributions to the Bill & Melinda Gates Foundation (although these can be offered). The only requirement of pledgers is to allocate a majority of their wealth to improving a lot of others. Each pledger publishes a statement that described the reason to become involved in the Giving Pledge, and these individuals meet annually in an effort to share ideas. Furthermore, Buffett and the Gates family have met with international philanthropists to learn about global perspectives as well as share ideas of what has been effective in the United States, with some non-U.S. pledgers such as Richard Branson of the Virgin Group.[43]

In Bill and Melinda's pledge letter to the Giving Pledge, they discuss the good fortune they have encountered but also the reasons for being involved in the giving pledge. Like many philanthropists before, Bill and Melinda Gates had multiple aims in their personal philanthropic efforts. One of those initiatives was education in the United States, which had been a subject of philanthropy among other business magnates like Carnegie, Rockefeller, and Vanderbilt in their own days. As they write, "We have visited schools that are breaking down old barriers and preparing every child for college and life. These are great schools—but there are not nearly enough of them. Now the task is to make sure that every student gets the same opportunity to succeed in college and life."[44]

For Bill Gates, the focus on college and postsecondary education is noteworthy: a highly intelligent and driven college dropout—who never returned to complete college—recognizing the value of this experience for workers in the current economy. The Gates family actively seeks educational reforms, both for the entire educational system and for training students for advanced careers in STEM disciplines (science, technology, engineering, and mathematics). Graduates in STEM disciplines are necessary to continue innovation and have been a subject Gates has often spoken about in the past.

The second major initiative within the Gates pledge letter is that of global public health, especially in regards to preventable diseases. The family wrote of reading about a preventable disease called rotavirus, which was killing 500,000 children worldwide every year and found this statistic unacceptable. Not only were the goals to help stop preventable deaths but also to ensure that proper health and education would allow children worldwide to grow to adulthood and have the opportunity to accomplish their own goals.

At the beginning of the year 2014, there were 115 billionaire individuals or families who had made a public commitment through the Giving Pledge, including familiar names such as:

Paul G. Allen—Microsoft cofounder, with Bill Gates

Sara Blakely—Spanx founder

Arthur M. Blank—Home Depot cofounder and owner of the Atlanta Falcons

Joan and **Richard Branson**—Founder of the Virgin Group

Warren Buffett—Berkshire Hathaway chairman and CEO

Jean and **Steve Case**—Former AOL CEO and Chairman

Larry Ellison—Oracle CEO

Reed Hastings and Patty Quinlan—Founder of LinkedIn

Carl Icahn—Investor and businessman

George Lucas—Producer /Director of *Star Wars* and *Indiana Jones* series

Dustin Moscovitz and Cari Tuna—Cofounder of Facebook

Elon Musk—Former CEO of PayPal, current CEO of Tesla Motors and SpaceX

Jeff Skoll—First president of eBay

Ted Turner—Founder of WTBS, CNN, and owner of the Atlanta Braves

Mark Zuckerberg—Cofounder and CEO of Facebook[45]

GLOBAL IMPROVEMENT

Through the combination of the Bill and Melinda Gates Foundation and the Giving Pledge, the Gates family has shown a clear effort to use wealth and influence not to simply become more influential, but to derive solutions that will benefit society. Although the Bill and Melinda Gates Foundation is expected to be extinguished shortly after the deaths of the couple, the Giving Pledge is designed to allow future billionaires to make the same commitment toward those who are less fortunate, for the projects that speak most to the ambitions of the donor. These programs are all voluntary, but the donors are making a difference like the wealthiest a century ago, much as Carnegie had when he funded the construction of what became almost half of the libraries in existence in the United States. In the case of the Gates family, their wealth is dedicated to the improvement of lives of others throughout the globe, either by promoting educational opportunity or by innovating and providing life-saving opportunities at the lowest cost, to simply provide the most good.

CONCLUSION

The story of Bill Gates is far from finished. Leading Microsoft as CEO from the earliest days of the micro-computing era until 2000, he re-shaped the way computers could be used by the average citizen—those without the technical sophistication he possesses—often calling for additional simplicity in the products that his firm developed. Leaving full-time work at Microsoft in 2008, thirty-three years into the company's history yet he was still just 52, he was able to commit his wealth in a meaningful attempt to save lives throughout the world. Even still, he was able to collaborate with Warren Buffett to have over 100 other billionaires commit to using more than half of their wealth for a phil-anthropic initiative of that donor's choosing.

Gates's success was not without challenges and controversy, and he was gifted at overcoming a number of potential hazards through an ability to reshape himself from an exceptionally brilliant early pro-grammer to an astute businessman who understood the potential of his staff to revolutionize computing. Life was not easy for his staff, and Gates has flaws and a drive that were sometimes to the detriment of his organization. He was able to lead Microsoft through a phase of tre-mendous growth and reach the pinnacle of the software market yet consistently believed his firm could fail. He was an early advocate for strong copyright rights for computer programs and understood that the market would pick the winner, simultaneously working on multiple similar projects before knowing which way the market would lead.

Once Windows 3.0 was released and sales quickly outpaced OS/2, he knew the path for operating systems was set, and the firm was free to focus on applications, such as Microsoft Office. His evolving relationship with Steve Jobs was one of admiration and friendship, despite times of friction with Apple (and even once being sued by Apple). In the post-Microsoft era, he's pursued various other business interests that help support his need for engagement as well as provide additional wealth to be donated through the Bill and Melinda Gates Foundation.

In the decades to come, Gates will once again find a way to surprise us all, whether through ideas generated at Microsoft, major breakthroughs made by the Foundation, or a new initiative of his choosing. The announcement in February 2014 that he would once again spend more time at Microsoft to mentor the new CEO of the firm, Satya Nadella, means that he is entering a new era of shaping a firm founded back in 1975, when he was just 19. Yet the work of the Foundation continues. As he once stated, if he were a teenager again, he would probably be "biology hacking" to solve problems throughout the world. Don't be surprised if a Gates protégé does this very thing one day during our lifetimes.

NOTES

CHAPTER 1

1. CNBC Town Hall Event: Warren Buffett and Bill Gates: Keeping America Great, November 12, 2009, at Columbia University.

2. Bill Gates Sr. and Mary Ann Mackin (2009). *Showing Up for Life: Thoughts on the Gifts of a Lifetime*. Broadway Books.

3. Andy Serwer (June 22, 2009). *Fortune*. Best Advice: Gates on Gates.

4. University of Washington (September 1995). Son Gives UW $10 Million in Honor of Mary Gates; Old Physics Building Renamed Mary Gates Hall. http://www.washington.edu/alumni/columns/sept95/gates_hall.html

5. *New York Times* (June 11, 1994). Mary Gates, 64; Helped Her Son Start Microsoft.

6. Bill Gates Sr. and Mary Ann Mackin (2009). *Showing Up for Life: Thoughts on the Gifts of a Lifetime*. Broadway Books.

7. Robert Guth (April 25, 2009). *Wall Street Journal*. Raising Bill Gates.

8. Bill Gates Sr. and Mary Ann Mackin (2009). *Showing Up for Life: Thoughts on the Gifts of a Lifetime*. Broadway Books.

9. Andy Serwer (June 22, 2009). *Fortune*. Best Advice: Gates on Gates.

10. Robert Guth (April 25, 2009). *Wall Street Journal*. Raising Bill Gates.

11. Walter Isaacson (June 24, 2001). *Time*. In Search of the Real Bill Gates.

12. Robert Guth (April 25, 2009). *Wall Street Journal*. Raising Bill Gates.

13. Bill Gates Sr. and Mary Ann Mackin (2009). *Showing Up for Life: Thoughts on the Gifts of a Lifetime*. Broadway Books.

14. PBS NOW: Bill Moyer Interviews Bill Gates. http://www.pbs .org/now/printable/transcript_gates_print.html.

15. Kristianne Blake—*Forbes*. http://www.forbes.com/profile/kristi anne-blake/.

16. Stuart Glascock (June 2013). *Columns: The University of Washington Alumni Magazine*. Mighty Is the Man Who Wears the Purple and Gold: The Immense Impact of Bill Gates Sr.

17. Ibid.

18. Sherry Grindeland (October 27, 1997). *Seattle Times*. Heartbreak Now a Mission—Libby Gates Armintrout to Speak about Breast Cancer.

19. Pomona Today (Spring 2006). *Pomona College Magazine*. Armintrout Joins Board.

CHAPTER 2

1. Michael D. Eisner with Aaron Cohen (2010). *Working Together: Why Great Partnerships Succeed*. Harper Business.

2. Andy Serwer (June 22, 2009). *Fortune*. Best Advice: Gates on Gates.

3. Robert X. Cringely (1996). *Accidental Empires*. HarperBusiness.

4. Bill Gates with Nathan Myhrvold and Peter Rinearson (1995). *The Road Ahead*. Viking.

5. David Allison (1993). Transcript of a Video History Interview with Mr. William "Bill" Gates. http://americanhistory.si.edu/comphist /gates.htm.

6. Andy Serwer (June 22, 2009). *Fortune*. Best Advice: Gates on Gates.

7. Alan Hughes (October 21, 2011). *Black Enterprise*. Can Bill Gates Save Our Schools?

8. Steven Levy (2010). *Hackers: Heroes of the Computer Revolution.* O'Reilly.

9. Bill Gates with Nathan Myhrvold and Peter Rinearson (1995). *The Road Ahead.* Viking.

10. Bill Gates (October 27, 2011). Early Days as a Computer Programmer. http://mobile.thegatesnotes.com/Personal/Early-Days-as-a-Computer-Programmer.

11. New Mexico Museum of Natural History and Science. *Traf-O-Data.* http://startup.nmnaturalhistory.org/gallery/story.php?ii=45.

12. Bill Gates Sr. and Mary Ann Mackin (2009). *Showing Up for Life: Thoughts on the Gifts of a Lifetime.* Broadway Books.

13. Bill Gates, Paul Allen, and Brent Schlender (October 2, 2005). *Fortune.* Bill Gates and Paul Allen Talk: Check Out the Ultimate Buddy Act in Business History. http://money.cnn.com/magazines/ fortune/ fortune_archive/1995/10/02/206528/.

14. Robert Guth (April 25, 2009). *Wall Street Journal.* Raising Bill Gates.

15. Andy Serwer (June 22, 2009). *Fortune.* Best Advice: Gates on Gates.

16. Bill Gates (June 7, 2007). Remarks of Bill Gates, Harvard Commencement 2007.

17. Jeffrey Young (January 27, 2007). *Forbes.* The George S. Patton of Software.

18. Malcolm Gladwell (2008). *Outliers: The Story of Success.* Hachette Book Group.

19. H. Edward Roberts and William Yates (February 1975). *Popular Electronics.* Build the Altair 8800 Minicomputer Part II.

20. U.S. Department of Labor Wage and Hour Division (WHD). History of Federal Minimum Wage Rates under the Fair Labor Standards Act, 1938–2009. http://www.dol.gov/whd/minwage/chart.htm# footnote.

21. Brent Schlender, Warren Buffett, and Bill Gates (July 20, 1998). *Fortune.* The Bill & Warren Show.

22. New Mexico Museum of Natural History and Science (n.d.). We Have a BASIC. http://startup.nmnaturalhistory.org/gallery/story. php?ii=20&sid=4.

23. Bill Gates (May/June 1977). *The Software Column.* Personal Computing, Volume 1.

24. Susan Lammers (1986). *Programmers at Work: Interviews with 19 Programmers Who Shaped the Computer Industry.* Tempus Books.

25. Bill Gates with Nathan Myhrvold and Peter Rinearson (1996). *The Road Ahead: Completely Revised and Up-to-Date.* Penguin.

26. Robert Slater (2004). *Microsoft Rebooted: How Bill Gates and Steve Ballmer Reinvented Their Company.* Penguin.

27. Robert X. Cringely (1996). *Triumph of the Nerds: The Rise of Accidental Empires.* PBS.

28. Paul Allen (May 2011). *Vanity Fair.* Microsoft's Odd Couple.

29. Bill Gates with Nathan Myhrvold and Peter Rinearson (1996). *The Road Ahead: Completely Revised and Up-to-Date.* Penguin.

30. Daniel Golden and John Yemma (March 31, 1998). *Boston Globe.* Harvard Amasses a $13b Endowment.

31. Bill Gates Sr. and Mary Ann Mackin (2009). *Showing Up for Life: Thoughts on the Gifts of a Lifetime.* Broadway Books.

32. Daniel Golden and John Yemma (March 31, 1998). *Boston Globe.* Harvard Amasses a $13b Endowment.

33. Ibid.

34. Bill Gates (June 7, 2007). Remarks of Bill Gates, Harvard Commencement 2007.

CHAPTER 3

1. Brent Schlender, Warren Buffett, and Bill Gates (July 20, 1998). *Fortune.* The Bill & Warren Show.

2. Paul E. Ceruzzi (July 2010). *OAH Magazine of History.* "Ready or Not, Computers Are Coming to the People": Inventing the PC.

3. CNBC Town Hall Event: Warren Buffett and Bill Gates: Keeping America Great, November 12, 2009, at Columbia University.

4. H. W. Brands (1999). *Masters of Enterprise.* Free Press.

5. Brent Schlender, Warren Buffett, and Bill Gates (July 20, 1998). *Fortune.* The Bill & Warren Show.

6. David Allison (1993). Transcript of a Video History Interview with Mr. William "Bill" Gates. http://americanhistory.si.edu/comphist /gates.htm.

7. Jeffrey A. Krames (2003). *What the Best CEOs Know: 7 Exceptional Leaders and Their Lessons for Transforming Any Business.* McGraw-Hill.

8. Robert X. Cringely (1996). *Accidental Empires*. HarperBusiness

9. Robert X. Cringely (1996). *Triumph of the Nerds: The Rise of Accidental Empires*. PBS.

10. Steven Levy (September 19, 2000). *Newsweek*. A Big Birthday for Bill & Co.

11. Bill Gates, Paul Allen, and Brent Schlender (October 2, 2005). *Fortune*. Bill Gates and Paul Allen Talk: Check Out the Ultimate Buddy Act in Business History. http://money.cnn.com/magazines/fortune/ fortune_archive/1995/10/02/206528/.

12. Steven Levy (2010). *Hackers: Heroes of the Computer Revolution*. O'Reilly.

13. Bill Gates (1976). *Open Letter to Hobbyists*. Computer Notes, Volume 1, Issue 9.

14. Randy Burge (November 16, 2006). The 1975 Popular Electronics Magazine That Inspired Paul Allen. http://www.abqtrib.com/news/2006 /nov/16/randy-burge-1975-popular-electronics-magazine-insp/.

15. Paul Allen (May 2011). *Vanity Fair*. Microsoft's Odd Couple.

16. Bill Gates (1977). *Popular Computing, Volume 1*, page 38.

17. Robert X. Cringely (1996). *Accidental Empires*. HarperBusiness.

18. Stephen Manes and Paul Andrews (1993). *Gates: How Microsoft's Mogul Reinvented an Industry—and Made Himself the Richest Man in America*. Doubleday.

19. Jeff Greene (2008). The "Albuquerque Photo." Microsoft Archives. http://blogs.msdn.com/b/prophoto/archive/2008/12/30/the-albuquerque-photo.aspx.

20. Stephen Manes and Paul Andrews (1993). *Gates: How Microsoft's Mogul Reinvented an Industry—and Made Himself the Richest Man in America*. Doubleday.

21. Transcript of Interview with Dennis Bathory-Kitsz (1980). B. Gates Rants about Software Copyrights—in 1980. http://features-beta .slashdot.org/story/00/01/20/1316236/b-gates-rants-about-software-copyrights---in-1980.

22. Dennis Bathory-Kitsz (1980). *80 Microcomputing*. Have the Courts Smashed Software Copyright?

23. Ibid.

24. David Allison (1993). Transcript of a Video History Interview with Mr. William "Bill" Gates. http://americanhistory.si.edu/comphist /gates.htm.

25. Michael D. Eisner with Aaron Cohen (2010). *Working Together: Why Great Partnerships Succeed*. Harper Business.

26. Richard Waters (November 1, 2013). *Financial Times*. An Exclusive Interview with Bill Gates.

27. David Lieberman (April 30, 2007). *USA Today*. CEO Forum: Microsoft's Ballmer Having a "Great" Time.

28. Robert Slater (2004). *Microsoft Rebooted: How Bill Gates and Steve Ballmer Reinvented Their Company*. Penguin.

29. Jessica Mintz (June 27, 2008). *Huff Post Business*. Bill Gates' Last Day at Microsoft: Bids Steve Ballmer Farewell in Tears.

30. Randall E. Stross (1997). *The Microsoft Way*. Addison-Wesley.

31. Robert X. Cringely (1996). *Accidental Empires*. HarperBusiness.

32. H. W. Brands (1999). *Masters of Enterprise*. Free Press.

33. *New York Times* (June 11, 1994). Mary Gates, 64; Helped Her Son Start Microsoft.

34. Robert X. Cringely (1996). *Accidental Empires*. HarperBusiness.

35. Purchase Agreement for Q-DOS from Seattle Computer Products by Microsoft.

36. Sample addendum listed in the Purchase Agreement for Q-DOS from Seattle Computer Products.

37. Walter Isaacson (2011). *Steve Jobs*. Simon & Schuster.

38. IBM Corporation (August 12, 1981). Press Release for the IBM-PC.

39. Robert X. Cringely (1996). *Accidental Empires*. HarperBusiness.

40. Paul Freiberger (August 31, 1981). *InfoWorld*. Bugs in TRS-80 Model III: How Bad Are They?

41. Lakeside School (n.d.). *Distinguished Alumni Award Recipients*. http://www.lakesideschool.org/ftpimages/252/download/Distinguished%20Alumni%20Award%20Recipients.pdf.

42. Paul Allen (May 2011). *Vanity Fair*. Microsoft's Odd Couple.

43. Paulina Borsook (February 2008). *Wired*. Accidental Billionaire.

44. Bill Gates and Steve Ballmer (1983). Microsoft Applications Strategy Memo.

45. David Allison (1993). Transcript of a Video History Interview with Mr. William "Bill" Gates. http://americanhistory.si.edu/comphist/gates.htm.

46. *Apple Computer, Inc. v. Franklin Computer Corporation* (August 30, 1983). U.S. Court of Appeals Third Circuit. http://digital-law-online.info/cases/219PQ113.htm.

47. William H. Gates (September 23, 1983). *New York Times*. Insurance for the Industry's Future.

48. Walter Isaacson (2011). *Steve Jobs*. Simon & Schuster.

49. Bill Gates with Nathan Myhrvold and Peter Rinearson (1995). *The Road Ahead*. Viking.

CHAPTER 4

1. *PC Magazine* (May 14, 1985). *Top-Bachelor Gates: Is he Compatible?*

2. OS/2 Joint Development Agreement between IBM and Microsoft.

3. Microsoft (November 2013). *A History of Windows*. http://windows.microsoft.com/en-us/windows/history#T1=era0.

4. Siegel—ABC News, How Steve Jobs Got Fired from His Own Company.

5. Bro Uttal (July 21, 1986). *Fortune*. Inside the Deal That Made Bill Gates $350,000,000.

6. P. McNamara (March 10, 2011). If You Had Bought 100 Shares of Microsoft 25 Years Ago . . . http://www.networkworld.com/community/blog/if-you-had-bought-100-shares-microsoft-25-yea.

7. Iacobucci, Ed. (1988). *OS/2 Programmer's Guide: Foreword*.

8. Jim Carlton (1997). *Apple: The Inside Story of Intrigue, Egomania, and Business Blunders*. Times Business.

9. *Success* magazine (October 1988). Lessons from a New-Product Wizard. http://www.success.com/article/lessons-from-a-new-product-wizard#sthash.07xQo8ag.dpuf.

10. Robert X. Cringely (1996). *Triumph of the Nerds: The Rise of Accidental Empires*. PBS.

11. Kurt Eichenwald (August 2012). *Vanity Fair*. Microsoft's Lost Decade.

12. Kathy Rebello, Evan I. Schwartz, John W. Verity, Mark Lewyn, Jonathan Levin (February 28, 1993). *BusinessWeek*. Is Microsoft Too Powerful?

13. Ibid.

14. Jeffrey A. Krames (2003). *What the Best CEOs Know: 7 Exceptional Leaders and Their Lessons for Transforming any Business*. McGraw-Hill.

15. Bill Gates (1995). The Internet Tidal Wave Memo. http://www.justice.gov/atr/cases/exhibits/20.pdf

16. Ibid.

17. Robert X. Cringely (1996). *Accidental Empires*. HarperBusiness.

18. Miguel Helft (January 2, 2014). *CNN/Money*. Microsoft's Chromebook Headache.

19. David Segal (August 24, 1995). *Washington Post*. With Windows 95's Debut, Microsoft Scales Heights of Hype.

20. Harry McCracken (May 07, 2013). *Time*. A Brief History of Windows Sales Figures 1985–Present. http://techland.time.com/2013/05/07/a-brief-history-of-windows-sales-figures-1985-present/.

21. Bill Gates with Nathan Myhrvold and Peter Rinearson (1996). *The Road Ahead: Completely Revised and Up-to-Date*. Penguin.

22. David Bank (February 1, 1999). *Wall Street Journal*. How Microsoft Wound Up in a Civil War Over Windows.

23. Walter Isaacson (June 24, 2001). *Time*. In Search of the Real Bill Gates.

24. Roben Farzad (December 9, 2013). *BusinessWeek*. Microsoft's Apple Investment: The Worst Deal of Them All? www.businessweek.com/articles/2103-12-09/worst-deal-ever-microsofts-apple-investment.

25. Rick Webb (November 12, 2011). *Betabeat*. Caught in the Webb: Let's Not Party Like It's 1999.

26. Microsoft (August 6, 1997). Microsoft and Apple Affirm Commitment to Build Next Generation Software for Macintosh.

27. Laurence Zuckerman (October 27, 1997). *New York Times*. New Jet Eases Travel Hassles for Bill Gates.

28. Bill Gates (November 14, 2007). Comments at Microsoft 2007 Annual Shareholder Meeting.

29. Ibid.

30. Bill Gates (1999). *Business @ the Speed of Thought: Using a Digital Nervous System*. Warner Books.

31. Walter Isaacson (June 24, 2001). *Time*. In Search of the Real Bill Gates.

32. Kurt Eichenwald (August 2012). *Vanity Fair.* Microsoft's Lost Decade.

33. Corey Grice and Sandeep Junnakar (July 2, 1998). *CNET News.* Gates, Buffett a bit Bearish.

34. Microsoft (n.d.). Microsoft Software Asset Management Policy. http://www.microsoft.com/sam/en/us/intproperty.aspx.

35. Corey Grice and Sandeep Junnakar (July 2, 1998). *CNET News.* Gates, Buffett a bit Bearish.

36. *Newsweek* Staff (June 22, 1997). *Newsweek.* How We Did It.

37. Michael D. Eisner with Aaron Cohen (2010). *Working Together: Why Great Partnerships Succeed.* Harper Business.

38. David Lieberman (April 30, 2007). *USA Today.* CEO Forum: Microsoft's Ballmer Having a "Great" Time.

CHAPTER 5

1. C. K. Prahalad and Gary Hamel (May–June 1990). *Harvard Business Review.* The Core Competence of the Corporation.

CHAPTER 6

1. Daniel Gross (1997). *Forbes Greatest Business Stories of All Time.* Wiley.

2. Steve Lohr (November 11, 1998). *New York Times.* Gates Quoted as Seeing Case "Blow Over."

3. Steve Lohr (August 22, 1995). *New York Times.* Judge Clears Antitrust Pact for Microsoft. http://www.nytimes.com/1995/08/22 /business/judge-clears-antitrust-pact-for-microsoft.html.

4. Matt Schudel (June 15, 2013). *Washington Post.* Thomas Penfield Jackson, Federal Judge, Dies at 76.

5. Steve Lohr (August 22, 1995). *New York Times.* Judge Clears Antitrust Pact for Microsoft. http://www.nytimes.com/1995/08/22 /business/judge-clears-antitrust-pact-for-microsoft.html.

6. Ibid.

7. Contempt Order for Violating First Consent Decree (1997). http://www.justice.gov/atr/cases/f1200/1236.htm.

8. Andrew Osterland (1996). *Financial World.* The Case against Microsoft.

9. Joe Belfiore (March 3, 1998). Internet Standards and Operating Systems—Why Integration Makes Sense. http://technet.microsoft.com/en-us/library/dd316500.aspx.

10. Ibid.

11. Brent Schlender, Warren Buffett, and Bill Gates (July 20, 1998). *Fortune*. The Bill & Warren Show.

12. Senate Judiciary Committee Record of Market Power and Structural Change in the Software Industry Hearing.

13. Dawn Kawamoto (August 28, 1998). *CNET News*. Gates Deposition Called Evasive.

14. Department of Justice Antitrust Website, http://www.justice.gov/atr/cases/ms_depos.htm.

15. Ellen Neuborne and Steve Hamm (November 30, 1998). *BusinessWeek*. Microsoft's Teflon Bill: So far, the Antitrust Trial Hasn't Sullied the Gates "Brand."

16. Matt Schudel (June 15, 2013). *Washington Post*. Thomas Penfield Jackson, Federal Judge, Dies at 76.

17. Joseph Nocera (April 26, 1999). *Fortune*. Microsoft and Me: With the Trial on Hold, Talk of a Settlement Emerges. Our Diarist Heads to Redmond to See if the Defendant Really Has Compromise in Mind.

18. Ken Auletta (2001). *World War 3.0: Microsoft and Its Enemies*. Random House.

19. Steven Levy (August 30, 1999). *Newsweek*. Behind the Gates Myth.

20. H. W. Brands (1999). *Masters of Enterprise*. Free Press.

21. Steve Lohr (March 11, 1999). *New York Times*. Microsoft Lawyer's Assessment of Trial: Not to Worry.

22. Ken Auletta (2001). *World War 3.0: Microsoft and Its Enemies*. Random House.

23. Judge Jackson's Findings of Fact, http://www.justice.gov/atr/cases/f3800/msjudgex.htm#iii.

24. Ibid.

25. Ibid.

26. Ken Auletta (2001). *World War 3.0: Microsoft and Its Enemies*. Random House.

27. Judge Jackson's Findings of Fact, http://www.justice.gov/atr/cases/f3800/msjudgex.htm#iii.

28. Ibid.

29. Ibid.

30. Bill Gates, Reactions to the Findings. http://online.wsj.com/article/SB941852551455642819.html?dsk=y.

31. Ken Auletta (2001). *World War 3.0: Microsoft and Its Enemies.* Random House.

32. Steve Young (May 22, 2000). *CNNfn.* Microsoft Renews Attack.

33. Ibid.

34. Final Judgment of June 7, 2000, http://www.gpo.gov/fdsys/pkg/GPO-USVMS/pdf/GPO-USVMS-2.pdf.

35. Ibid.

36. Memorandum and Order of June 7, 2000, http://www.justice.gov/atr/cases/f219700/219731.htm.

37. Ibid.

38. David Kleinbard and Richard Richtmyer (June 7, 2000). *CNNfn.* Judge Orders Microsoft Split.

39. Andrew Stephen (2000). *New Statesman.* Gates Loses $12bn, Just Like That.

40. Proposed Findings of Fact, Section VII—http://www.justice.gov/atr/cases/f2600/2613b_htm.htm.

41. N. Petreley (2000). *Infoworld.* This Year's Award for Industry Achievement Goes to the Creator of Linux, Linus Torvalds.

42. Berkman Center for Internet & Society (February 28, 2001). http://cyber.law.harvard.edu/node/279.

43. Ken Auletta (January 15, 2001). *The New Yorker.* Final Offer.

44. Ibid.

45. Stephen Labaton (February 28, 2001). *New York Times.* Judges Voice Doubt on Order Last Year to Split Microsoft.

46. Memorandum from Judge Jackson of March 12, 2001.

47. Ibid.

48. Ibid.

49. Ken Auletta (January 15, 2001). *The New Yorker.* Final Offer.

50. Final Judgment by Judge Colleen Kollar-Kotelly, http://www.justice.gov/atr/cases/f200400/200457.htm.

2. Deborah Solomon (2010). *New York Times*. The Donor: Questions for Melinda Gates.

3. Robert Slater (2004). *Microsoft Rebooted: How Bill Gates and Steve Ballmer Reinvented Their Company*. Penguin.

4. Bill Gates Sr. and Mary Ann Mackin (2009). *Showing Up for Life: Thoughts on the Gifts of a Lifetime*. Broadway Books.

5. Michael Newman (May 23, 1999). *Pittsburgh Post-Gazette*. Bob Is Dead; Long Live Bob.

6. Michael D. Eisner with Aaron Cohen (2010). *Working Together: Why Great Partnerships Succeed*. Harper Business.

7. Profile of Melinda French Gates (2013). *Forbes*. Third Most Powerful Woman.

8. R. Folkers (1998). *U.S. News & World Report*. Dear Diary: The Gates Files.

9. Paul Andrews (January 29, 1998). *Seattle Times*. Bill Gates Sings for Barbara Walters—Software Magnate to Show Softer Side—And a New Talent—on National TV.

10. Deborah Solomon (2010). *New York Times*. The Donor: Questions for Melinda Gates.

11. Walter Isaacson (June 24, 2001). *Time*. In Search of the Real Bill Gates.

12. Caroline Graham (June 9, 2011). *Daily Mail*. This Is Not the Way I'd Imagined Bill Gates . . . A Rare and Remarkable Interview with the World's Second Richest Man. http://www.dailymail.co.uk/home/moslive/article-2001697/Microsofts-Bill-Gates-A-rare-remarkable-interview-worlds-second-richest-man.html.

13. Ibid.

14. Zillow (June 25, 2013). Bill Gates Buys Equestrian Estate in Florida for $8.7 Million. http://www.forbes.com/sites/zillow/2013/06/25/bill-gates-buys-equestrian-estate-in-florida-for-8–7-million/.

15. Caroline Graham (June 9, 2011). *Daily Mail*. This Is Not the Way I'd Imagined Bill Gates . . . A Rare and Remarkable Interview with the World's Second Richest Man. http://www.dailymail.co.uk/home/moslive/article-2001697/Microsofts-Bill-Gates-A-rare-remarkable-interview-worlds-second-richest-man.html.

16. Danny Westneat (March 8, 2011). *Seattle Times*. Bill Gates, Have I Got a Deal for You! http://seattletimes.com/html/dannywestneat/2014437975_danny09.html.

17. Mary Riddell (January 27, 2012). *The Telegraph*. Bill Gates: "I Wrote Steve Jobs a Letter as He Was Dying. He Kept It by His Bed." http://www.telegraph.co.uk/technology/bill-gates/9041726/Bill-Gates-I-wrote-Steve-Jobs-a-letter-as-he-was-dying.-He-kept-it-by-his-bed.html.

18. Q&A for Bill Gates.

19. King County Property Tax Assessment (2014).

20. Bohlin Cywinski Jackson (n.d.). Pacific Rim Estate. http://www.bcj.com/public/projects/project/12.html.

21. Home Front (December 20, 1996). Bill Gates' Guest House Wins Architects' Award. http://online.wsj.com/news/articles/SB851011416867310000.

22. Bill Gates with Nathan Myhrvold and Peter Rinearson (1995). *The Road Ahead*. Viking.

23. Richard Folkers (November 23, 1997). *U.S. News and World Report*. Bill Gates's Stately Pleasure Dome and Futuristic Home. http://money.usnews.com/money/business-economy/articles/1997/11/23/xanadu-20?page=2.

24. Paul Andrews (January 29, 1998). *Seattle Times*. Bill Gates Sings for Barbara Walters—Software Magnate to Show Softer Side—and a New Talent—on National TV.

CHAPTER 10

1. Ben Mezrich (2009). *The Accidental Billionaires: The Founding of Facebook. A Tale of Sex, Money, Genius, and Betrayal*. Doubleday.

2. Zachary M. Seward (February 27, 2004). *Harvard Crimson*. Dropout Gates Drops into Talk.

3. Ben Mezrich (2009). *The Accidental Billionaires: The Founding of Facebook. A Tale of Sex, Money, Genius, and Betrayal*. Doubleday.

4. Nicholas D. Kristof and Sheryl WuDunn. (2010). *Half the Sky*. Vintage.

5. *USA Today* (December 14, 2004). Bill Gates Elected to Berkshire Hathaway Board.

6. Bill Gates (August 28, 2013). We Need Our Brightest People Working on Our Biggest Problems. http://www.linkedin.com/today/post/article/20130828134129-251749025-we-need-our-brightest-people-working-on-our-biggest-problems?trk=mp-reader-card.

7. Bill Gates (June 12, 2013). Three Things I've Learned from Warren Buffett. http://www.linkedin.com/today/post/article/2013061 2065727–251749025-three-things-i-ve-learned-from-warren-buf fett?trk=eml-mktg-celeb-bg-title.

8. Patrick Thibodeau (November 17, 2008). *Computerworld.* Gates Claims Cap on H-1B Visas Puts U.S. High-Tech Jobs at Risk.

9. http://www.secform4.com/filings/789019/000122520812002153. htm.

10. http://www.secform4.com/filings/789019/000122520813022807. htm - November 4.

11. Microsoft Inc. (February 2014). Microsoft Board Names Satya Nadella as CEO. http://www.microsoft.com/en-us/news/press/2014/ feb14/02-04newspr.aspx.

12. http://www.cpexecutive.com/regions/southwest/bill-gates-in vestment-group-buys-four-seasons-houston/ http://www.ajc.com/news/ business/four-seasons-hotel-atlanta-in-midtown-sold-for-62m/nbz5m/ http://www.seattlepi.com/business/tech/article/Bill-Gates-buying-Mexican-resort-5069752.php.

13. http://investors.autonation.com/phoenix.zhtml?c=85803 &p=irolgovBioBoard&ID=200270 http://finance.yahoo.com/q/mh?s= RSG+Major+Holders http://www.ecolab.com/our-story/our-company/ our-expertise-and-innovation.

14. David Roman and Christopher Bjork (October 22, 2013). *Wall Street Journal.* Bill Gates Buys Stake in Spanish Construction Company FCC. http://investors.morningstar.com/ownership/ shareholders-major.html?t=CNI http://investors.morningstar.com/ ownership/shareholders-major.html?t=DE&region=usa&culture=en-US&ownerCountry=USA.

15. Jack Witzig and Pamela Roux (May 28, 2013). *Bloomberg Personal Finance.* Bill Gates Fattens Wealth Gap over Slim as Cascade Surges. http://www.bloomberg.com/news/2013-05-29/bill-gates-fattens-wealth-gap-over-slim-as-cascade-surges.html.

16. Corbis Fact Sheet (n.d.). http://corporate.corbis.com/company-fact-sheet/.

17. Leslie Helm (April 2012). *Seattle Business Magazine.* Executive Q&A: Gary Shenk CEO, Corbis Corporation.

18. Natalie Apostolou (May, 16, 2012). *The Register*. Gates' Corbis Busted Again for Fraud. http://www.theregister.co.uk/2012/05/16/gates_fights_ex_employee/.

CHAPTER 11

1. Regina Hackett (May 19, 2005). *Seattle P-I*. Gates' Lawyer Failed to Gain Tax Exemption for da Vinci Documents.

2. Leonard Kniffel (December 2003). *American Libraries*. Bill Gates: Why He Did It.

3. Ibid.

4. Patricia Martin (September 1997). *American Libraries*. On My Mind: Is Bill Gates the New Andrew Carnegie?

5. JBHE (Autumn 1997). *Journal of Blacks in Higher Education*. Bill Gates and the Black Colleges.

6. Theodore Cross (Autumn 1999). *Journal of Blacks in Higher Education*. Bill Gate's Gift to Racial Preferences in Higher Education.

7. Gates Millennium Scholars Program, http://www.gmsp.org/publicweb/aboutus.aspx.

8. JBHE (Summer 2001). *Journal of Blacks in Higher Education*. Bill Gates Still Has More Financial Wealth Than Do All Black American Households Combined.

9. BBC News (January 5, 1999). "Pie Terrorists" Fined for Gates Attack. http://news.bbc.co.uk/2/hi/americas/249066.stm.

10. Nader Letter to Bill Gates requesting he initiate a billionaire's "National and Global Wealth Disparities and What to Do About It" event.

11. Gates Response to Nader, August 4, 1997.

12. Nader's Parting Shot after Gates Response of August 4, 1998.

13. Herbold's Response to Nader's "invitation" to the *Appraising Microsoft and Its Global Strategy* conference to be held during Microsoft's 1997 Shareholder Meeting, on the other side of the continent.

14. Jeri Clausing (November 14, 1997). *New York Times*. Nader Conference Levels Sights on Microsoft.

15. Oxfam Briefing Paper 178 (January 20, 2014). Working for a few. Oxfam made a calculation based upon the data in the Credit Suisse Report.

16. Robert Slater (2004). *Microsoft Rebooted: How Bill Gates and Steve Ballmer Reinvented Their Company*. Penguin.

17. Ibid.

18. Bill and Melinda Gates Foundation (n.d.). Foundation Factsheet. http://www.gatesfoundation.org/who-we-are/general-information/foundation-factsheet.

19. Bill and Melinda Gates Foundation (n.d.) Who We Are. http://www.gatesfoundation.org/Who-We-Are/General-Information/Letter-from-Bill-and-Melinda-Gates.

20. PBS NOW: Bill Moyers Interviews Bill Gates. http://www.pbs.org/now/printable/transcript_gates_print.html.

21. Ilona Kickbusch (2001). *Journal of Epidemiology and Community Health*. A Note to Bill Gates.

22. Ibid.

23. Michael Specter (October 24, 2005). *New Yorker*. What Money Can Buy: Millions of Africans Die Needlessly of Disease Each Year. Can Bill Gates Change That?

24. Bill Gates (June 7, 2007). Remarks of Bill Gates, Harvard Commencement 2007.

25. Bill Gates (January 24, 2008). Creative Capitalism Speech at Davos World Economic Forum, 2008.

26. Newsweek Staff (June 21, 2008). *Newsweek*. Microsoft after Gates (and Bill after Microsoft).

27. Todd Bishop and Tom Paulson (June 23, 2008). *Seattle P-I*. Q&A: Gates Talks About Letting Go, the Future and the Foundation. http://www.seattlepi.com/business/article/Q-A-Gates-talks-about-letting-go-the-future-and-1277371.php.

28. Steven Levy (June 21, 2008). *Newsweek*. Gates: Microsoft, the Suit and His Foundation.

29. Fareed Zakaria (October 5, 2008). *CNN*. Bill Gates Interview; Third World Development; Solving the Economic Crisis.

30. Steven Levy (2010). *Hackers: Heroes of the Computer Revolution*. O'Reilly.

31. Bill Gates (February 2009). *TED Talk*.

32. Michael D. Eisner with Aaron Cohen (2010). *Working Together: Why Great Partnerships Succeed*. Harper Business.

33. Mary Riddell (January 27, 2012). *The Telegraph.* Bill Gates: "I Wrote Steve Jobs a Letter as He Was Dying. He Kept It by His Bed." http://www.telegraph.co.uk/technology/bill-gates/9041726/Bill-Gates-I-wrote-Steve-Jobs-a-letter-as-he-was-dying.-He-kept-it-by-his-bed.html.

34. Bill Gates (April 28, 2013). Why We're Talking to Scientists about Toilets. http://mobile.thegatesnotes.com/Topics/Development/Talking-to-Scientists-About-Toilets.

35. Danielle Dellorto (February 4, 2011). *CNN.* Bill Gates: Vaccine-Autism Link "an Absolute Lie." http://www.cnn.com/2011/HEALTH/02/03/gupta.gates.vaccines.world.health/.

36. Gardiner Harris (February 2, 2010). *New York Times.* Journal Retracts 1998 Paper Linking Autism to Vaccines.

37. Valerie Strauss (November 27, 2013). *Washington Post.* Gates Foundation Pours Millions into Common Core in 2013.

38. *Bloomberg* (July 17, 2010). Gates' Latest Mission: Fixing America's Schools.

39. Brad Stone (August 8, 2013). *BusinessWeek.* Bill Gates on His Foundation's Health and Education Campaigns.

40. Bill and Melinda Gates (2014). Bill and Melinda Gates Foundation Annual Letter. http://annualletter.gatesfoundation.org/~/media/Annual%20Letter%202014/PDFs/2014_GatesAnnualLetter_ENGLISH_1.pdf.

41. Ibid.

42. Gates Family Pledge Letter (2010). The Giving Pledge. http://givingpledge.org/pdf/letters/Gates_Letter.pdf.

43. The Giving Pledge FAQ (n.d.). http://givingpledge.org/pdf/GivingPledge_FAQ.pdf.

44. Gates Family Pledge Letter (2010). The Giving Pledge. http://givingpledge.org/pdf/letters/Gates_Letter.pdf.

45. The Giving Pledge Letters Collection (2014). http://givingpledge.org/pdf/Pledge%20Letters%20Collection.pdf.

FURTHER READING

As a living subject, additional works are continually developed describing the life and new contributions of Bill Gates. A history is also maintained by the two organizations of which Bill Gates has been most influential:

- Microsoft: http://www.microsoft.com
- Bill and Melinda Gates Foundation: http://www.gatesfoundation.org/

Gates currently posts on the following media:

- The Gates Notes: http://www.thegatesnotes.com/
- LinkedIn: http://www.linkedin.com/in/williamhgates

Major documents by Bill Gates include:

- *The Open Letter to Hobbyists* (letter), 1976
- *Applications Strategy Memo* (memo to staff), 1983 with Steve Ballmer
- *The Internet Tidal Wave* (memo to staff), 1995

- *The Road Ahead* (book), 1995
- *The Road Ahead: Completely Revised and Up-to-Date* (book), 1996
- *Business @ the Speed of Thought: Using a Digital Nervous System* (book), 1999
- *The Trustworthy Computing Memo* (memo to staff), 2002

INDEX

Note: Italic page numbers indicate photos.

About the Author

DR. MICHAEL B. BECRAFT is the Edward F. Lyle Professor of Finance and Director of the Graduate Program in Business for the Park University School of Business, with an office location in Kansas City, Missouri.